Tim Winton's

Cloudstreet

Study notes for Advanced English
Second edition
Module B 2015–2020 HSC

Lewis Mitchell

Five Senses Education Pty Ltd
2/195 Prospect Highway
Seven Hills 2147
New South Wales
Australia

First Published 2008, Reprinted 2011, 2015

Mitchell, Lewis
Top Notes – Cloudstreet
ISBN 978-1-76032-061-4

CONTENTS

TOP NOTES SERIES

This series has been created to assist HSC students of English in their understanding of set texts. Top Notes are easy to read, providing analysis of issues and discussion of important ideas contained in the texts.

Particular care has been taken to ensure that students are able to examine each text in the context of the module it has been allocated to.

Each text generally includes:

- Notes on the specific module
- Plot summary
- Character analysis
- Setting
- Thematic concerns
- Language studies
- Essay questions and a modelled response
- Other textual material
- Study practice questions
- Useful quotes

I am sure you will find these Top Notes useful in your studies of English.

Bruce Pattinson
Series Editor

THE ADVANCED COURSE

This is a brief overview of the Advanced Course to ensure you are completely familiar with the different sections involved in the course. If in any doubt at all, check with your teacher or the Board of Studies.

The Advanced Course requires you to have studied:

- Five prescribed texts. This means five texts from the list given to your teacher by the Board of Studies.

- For each of the texts, **one** must come from **each** of the following five categories.

  - Shakespearian drama
  - prose fiction (novel usually)
  - drama or film
  - poetry
  - nonfiction or media or film or multimedia texts. (Multimedia are CD Roms, websites, etc.)

- A range of related texts of your own choosing. These are part of your Area of Study and Module C. Do not confuse these with the main set text you are studying and focusing on. This is very important.

Paper One

Area of Study: Discovery

Paper Two

Module A

Comparative Study of Texts and Context

Electives

- Intertextual Connections

OR

- Intertextual Perspectives

Module B

Critical Study of Text

- Prose Fiction

OR

- Shakespeare

OR

- Poetry

OR

- Drama or Film

OR

- Nonfiction, Media, Multimedia

Module C

Representation and Text

Electives

- Representing People and Politics

OR

- Representing People and Landscapes

You must study the Area of Study and EACH of Modules A, B and C

There are options within EACH of these that your school will select.

STUDYING A FICTION TEXT

The medium of any text is very important. If a text is a novel this must not be forgotten. Novels are *read*. This means you should refer to the "reader" but the "responder" can also be used when you are referring to the audience of the text.

The marker will want to know you are aware of the text as a novel and that you have considered its effect as a written text.

Remembering a fiction text is a written text also means when you are exploring *how* the composer represents his/her ideas you MUST discuss language techniques. This applies to any response you do using a novel, irrespective of the form the response is required to be in.

Language techniques are all the devices the author uses to represent his or her ideas. They are the elements of a fiction that are manipulated by authors to make any novel represent its ideas effectively! You might also see them referred to as stylistic devices or narrative techniques.

Every fiction text uses language techniques differently. Some authors have their own favourite techniques that they are known for such as symbolism or personification. Others use a variety to make their text achieve its purpose.

Some common language techniques are shown on the diagram that follows.

LANGUAGE TECHNIQUES

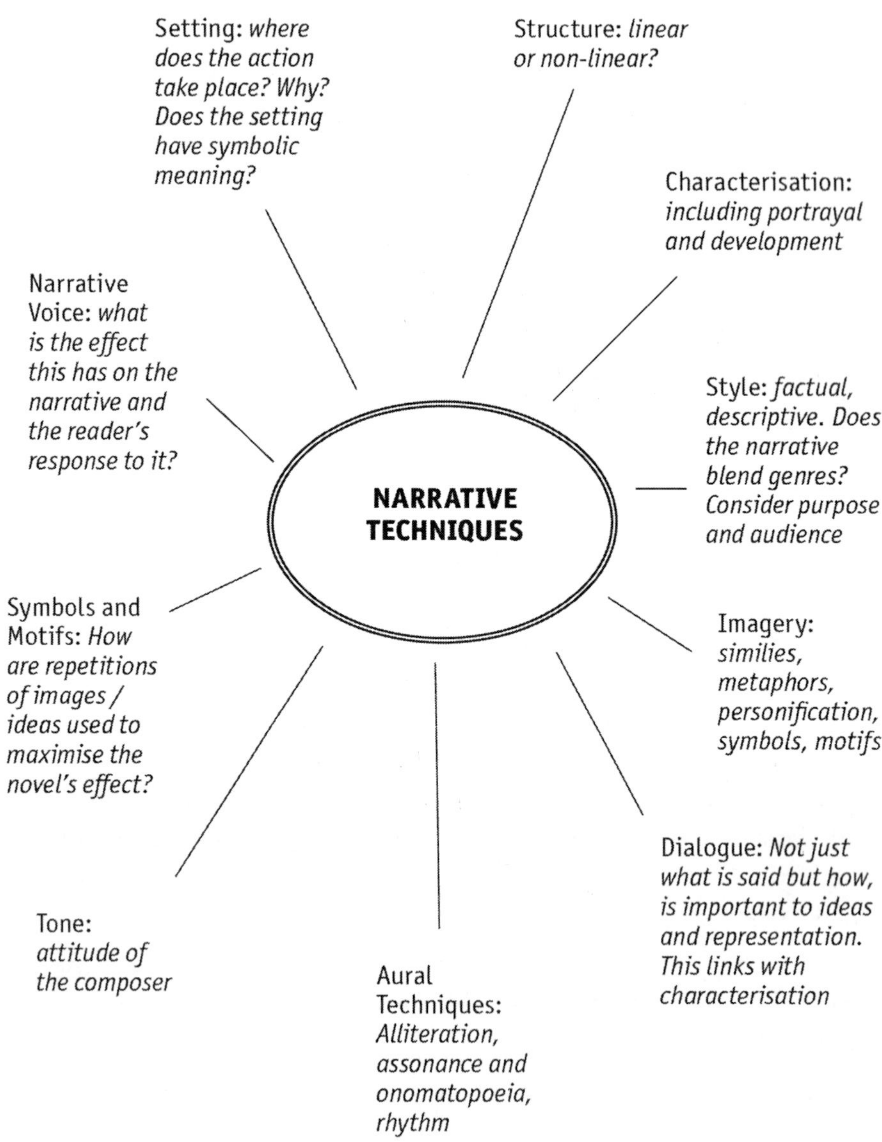

CRITICAL STUDY OF TEXT – SYLLABUS REQUIREMENTS

The Board of Studies documentation says of Module B: Critical Study of Texts that it:

> *"requires students to engage with and develop an informed personal understanding of their prescribed text."*

Throughout their study of this module students are required to:

- critically evaluate the language, content and construction of the prescribed text
- develop an appreciation of the textual integrity of the prescribed text
- critically evaluate the text in the light of other perspectives
- understand how the text has been received and valued.

Considering these requirements it is essential to examine each text in detail in order to develop an informed personal response and an understanding of how different ways of reading a text will influence an interpretation of it.

No related texts are required in this module.

CRITICAL STUDY OF TEXT

A critical study of a text requires the reader to engage in both critical theory and critical practice. Critical theory is concerned primarily with the questions that we ask about texts. These questions can be sorted into three main groups.

- What the text is about?
- How the text is constructed?
  and
- Why?

Critical practice is the process we go through in order to answer these questions.

It is also essential to assess and evaluate how our responses to a text are shaped by the context surrounding it and our reading of it. In order to do this a basic understanding of various critical theories and how these apply to texts is required.

Literary criticism may seem incredibly challenging, particularly if you have attempted to come to terms with some of the complex academic language and unfamiliar terminology often used to explain it. However, it is very similar to what you have always done as an Advanced English student. It extends on the basic practice of questioning the assumptions underpinning a text and acknowledging the role of the historical, cultural and social context of both the composer and responder in the construction of meaning in the text.

A critical study complements the more traditional approach to literary criticism, which valued the close analysis of the words on the page. However, it is important to understand that an in depth understanding of the language techniques and textual features of a text remains essential.

It is also imperative to note that different critical theories, and the ways of reading texts that have been developed from these, cannot be reduced to simple formulas to be applied to individual texts.

This module requires you to engage personally with each text set for study, analysing each rigorously in order to develop your own readings of them. Do not focus on critical readings but use them to inform your own ideas.

WAYS OF READING

The following is a summary of the ways of reading a text that have been applied throughout this study guide.

Dominant Reading

A dominant reading, otherwise known as an invited or a preferred reading of a text, is the most obvious, or literal reading of a text. This type of reading reflects the stereotypes dominant within the society to which it belongs. It favours the most dominant members of a culture, reflecting the values and attitudes of the figures of authority within it – for instance the media, leading businesses or the church.

When a dominant reading is opposed, and alternatives to the dominant values and attitudes present in the text are identified, a resistant reading occurs. When the reader chooses to accept part of the dominant ideology and challenge another part of it at the same time, this is referred to as an alternative reading.

Feminist Reading

A feminist reading of a text will focus on how women are represented in it, as well as the relationship between men and women. The relationships between texts are also significant in a feminist reading. In order to develop a feminist reading you will need to identify the assumptions of gender, noting that these could vary. Gender assumptions will relate both to the behaviour of the females in the text and their role in society.

Post-Modern Reading

A post-modern reading of a text will focus on how meaning is constructed through the connections between texts (intertextuality). Therefore post-modernism challenges the idea that meaning is a reflection of values. The distinction between popular culture and high art is also central to a post-modern approach to the reading of a text. Post-modern readings often challenge the concept of truth.

Freudian / Psychoanalytic Reading

A Freudian reading of a text will focus on how the emotions and thoughts of the persona / character in the text emerge out of their past experiences that have been repressed (not consciously dealt with). In addition, this type of reading might focus on the text as indicative of the author's needs and desires, both conscious and unconscious. Therefore, the psychological profile of the composer relates directly to the meaning of the text.

The role of language in how we understand ourselves and the world we live in is a central concern of more recent psychoanalytic theory. These theorists suggest that language, like the unconscious, contributes to a division between the world and how we see it and our actual self compared to how we see ourselves because there is always a gap between what is real and how it is named.

Therefore a psychoanalytic reading may focus on the role of dreams and memories, how these are dealt with in order to make meaning and what they suggest about the conscious and unconscious desires of the persona/composer. Similarly, the role of language in making sense of the world and notions of the self and identity will need to be considered.

Marxist Reading

A Marxist reading is concerned with the potential of a text to influence and control people through the values and beliefs it represents. Therefore a Marxist reading will evaluate how society is represented in a text. For instance, it might challenge a text by identifying the upper and middle-class values and beliefs it endorses. Therefore a Marxist reading will focus on and identify the perceptions and assumptions in the text that relate to class and the concept of power relations – including occupation, education, gender, age, race, rank and so on.

THE AUTHOR

Tim Winton was born in Perth in 1960. He is the author of over fourteen books, ranging from novels, non-fiction, short stories and books for children. He began writing when he was very young and his first novel, *An Open Swimmer*, won the Australian Vogel Prize in 1981.

Cloudstreet was published in 1991, winning the Miles Franklin Award that year. It was written mostly in France, suggesting that the author had to distance himself from Australia in order to write the quintessentially Australian novel. It is based on events in the lives of his own family, especially his grandparents and parents. You might note that the novel is dedicated to Winton's grandparents.

In 2003, the Australian Society of Authors compiled a list of the forty most popular Australian books of all time. There were three Winton novels in the list and *Cloudstreet* was rated first. When asked about this, Tim Winton replied with typical off-hand modesty: 'It's nice to be recognised by your peers, but I don't know if I'd be taking it as gospel.'

Although he grew up in the suburbs (of Perth in Western Australia), Winton has a love of the Australian landscape. He has described his characters as 'figures in landscape', indicating how important setting is in his novels. Many of his characters are on a quest for self-discovery. He has acknowledged that his characters become real to him – 'years later you'll have dreams about them.'

More recent novels *The Riders* and *Dirt Music* were both short-listed for the international Booker Prize. Winton's writing is loved for its warmth, humour and perceived characteristic 'Australianness'. He is almost certainly Australia's best-loved novelist.

Tim Winton lives in Western Australia with his wife and three children. He has a down-to-earth image and wears his hair in a long ponytail. He still loves to fish and surf.

CONTEXT

Cloudstreet was written in the late 1980s and early 1990s and published in 1991. The novel is set in the 1940s, 1950s and early 1960s. So here you have a novelist looking back to an era before his own generation.

Add to this the fact that we know that the novel is based on the lives of Winton's own grandparents and parents and you have a formula for nostalgia.

In addition, the novel was written while Winton was living in Europe, mostly in France. This is an author looking back in time and place.

Life in the novel is not depicted as easy, but the 'greed is good' heartlessness of the 1980s and the political instability of the Europe in which he was writing may well have helped to create a nostalgia for the past.

The novel shows a family sticking together against all odds, and in fact adopting another family at the end. Family, tolerance and a search for happiness in simple things characterise the philosophy behind the novel. These values can be contrasted with what Winton must have seen all around him as he was writing. This may help account for the popularity of the novel – it is about a time when Australia was more 'Australian' and more 'have a go' tolerant.

PLOT OUTLINE

Sam Pickles loses four fingers in an accident at work.

The black man appears at the door with stick props.

Fish Lamb drowns while fishing, but his mother revives him.

The war ends and Sam goes gambling.

Lester buys a boat and gets Quick and Fish to row it home.

Fish's brother Quick realizes that 'not all of Fish Lamb had come back.'

Oriel moves out of the house and into the tent.

The Pickles inherit Number One Cloud Street in the city and move in.

Quick runs away.

The Lambs rent half the house.

A rival shop opens, run by ex AIF G.M.Clay. Oriel takes him on and wins.

Oriel and Lester open a shop in the front room.

Rose gets a job in the city. She eats and puts on weight.

Fish is unable to recognise Oriel.

Oriel sees her life as hell. Ted leaves home. Fish yearns for the water.

Quick makes a living culling kangaroos.

He has to leave town when he is caught with the landowner's daughter.

A black man tries to lead him home but he goes to work for cousin Earl.

Quick glows so Earl and May take him home on Hat's wedding day.

Sam's gambling debts send him into hiding. Lester has an affair with Dolly.

Sam wins at two-up. Oriel takes Quick prawning.

Rose goes out with Toby Raven.

Rose leaves Toby and happens upon Quick and Fish on the river.

Rose and Quick are married. Oriel and Dolly dance together at the reception.

Quick joins the police force and Rose falls pregnant.

Ted dies and Rose has a miscarriage.

Dolly is grief stricken about Ted. She goes missing.

The police find her. She tells Rose about her incestuous background and they both weep.

The Nedlands Monster begins his murder spree.

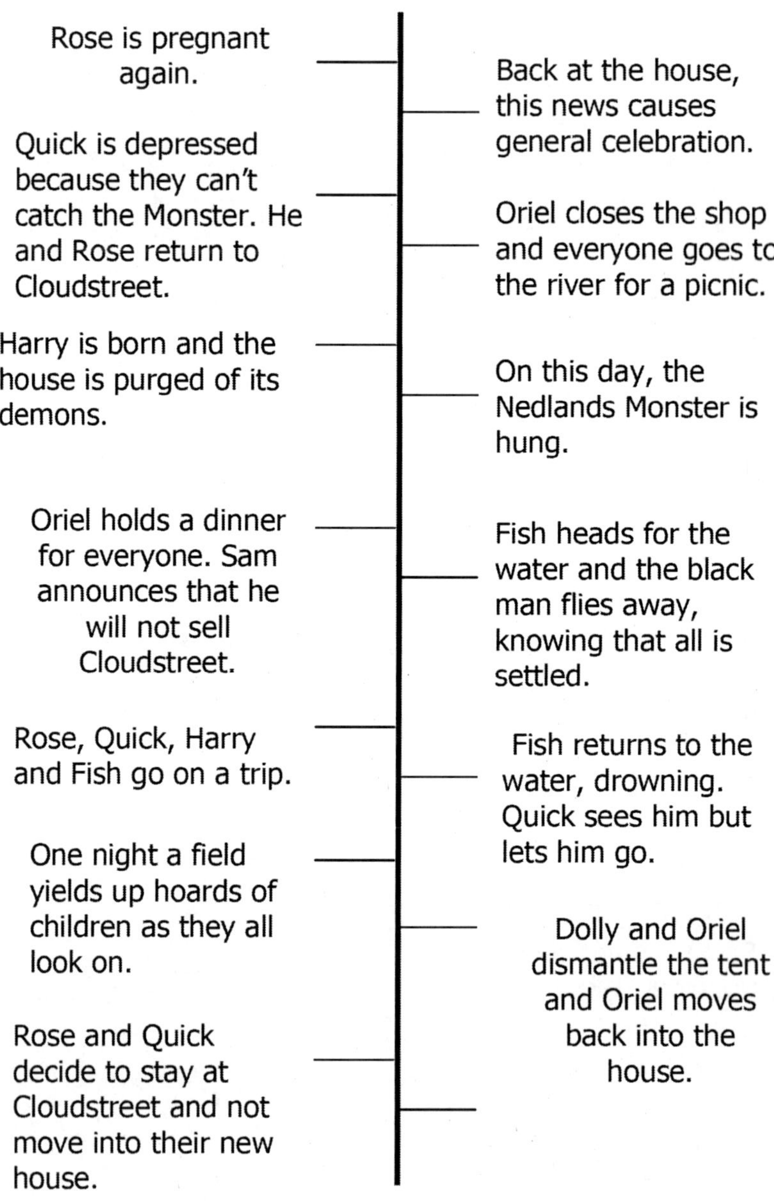
Rose is pregnant again.
Back at the house, this news causes general celebration.
Quick is depressed because they can't catch the Monster. He and Rose return to Cloudstreet.
Oriel closes the shop and everyone goes to the river for a picnic.
Harry is born and the house is purged of its demons.
On this day, the Nedlands Monster is hung.
Oriel holds a dinner for everyone. Sam announces that he will not sell Cloudstreet.
Fish heads for the water and the black man flies away, knowing that all is settled.
Rose, Quick, Harry and Fish go on a trip.
Fish returns to the water, drowning. Quick sees him but lets him go.
One night a field yields up hoards of children as they all look on.
Dolly and Oriel dismantle the tent and Oriel moves back into the house.
Rose and Quick decide to stay at Cloudstreet and not move into their new house.

PLOT SUMMARY

Cloudstreet is divided into ten numbered sections, usually referred to as chapters. Each of these chapters is made up of sections that aren't numbered but have titles. In addition there is an opening passage and a closing passage – these are often referred to as the prologue and the epilogue.

The Prologue

The novel opens with a description of a group of people having a picnic beside a river. It is 'an earthly vision', but 'even the missing are there'. So, the spirits of the dead are present as well as the living.

The focus turns to one of the living who is 'leaving'. He is drawn to the water and can't wait to be lost in it. For a moment he'll know the story – the moment of his dying. It is this moment of understanding that is captured in the 423 pages of the novel that follow.

Tim Winton uses 'second person' ('you') in the last paragraph to bring the reader into the scene and express the idea that this moment of death is one that we will all eventually experience. Also, we gradually comprehend the fact that the narrator spiritual Fish is talking to his other physical self.

Few readers will fully understand this prologue at first reading. It should be reread when you have finished the novel, in conjunction with p422 – 424 (*Moon, Sun, Stars*), which describes the same moment in time.

THE CHAPTERS

I

Rose Pickles is at the local swimming baths (pool) watching her brothers Ted and Chub swimming. 'She was a pretty kid, but not as pretty as her mother' (p 8), everyone told her. She has a feeling that something is about to go wrong.

Her father, Sam, is having the same feeling. He recalls that his own father believed deeply in luck, 'the shifty shadow of God is lurking'. At work, Sam loses all the fingers of his right hand in an accident with a winch.

Rose is sent to fetch her mother, Dolly. She finds her in the family's rented room at the pub, 'entertaining' a stranger. When she understands what has happened, Dolly curses that it is Sam's 'working hand'.

Sam settles into life as a cripple, but his successful (lucky) cousin Joel encourages him to get on with life. They go fishing, and 'lucky' Joel has a heart attack and dies.

II

The Lamb family are reversing their old Chev truck up a hill, because it can't make it forward in first gear. They are going prawning. Lester and Oriel Lamb are 'Godfearing people' with six children. Lester is working as a policeman because their farm is ruined.

Lester takes his two older sons out net-prawning with him. Mason (eleven years old) is known as 'Quick' because he is slow, rather like his father. Samson (nine) is known as 'Fish,' 'for his wit and alertness'. Everyone loves Fish.

Oriel has a sudden premonition, leaps up and cries out. Unnoticed by Lester or Quick, Fish goes down, under the net. Alarmed by Oriel's cry, Lester wheels around and knocks the lantern into the water, leaving them in darkness. Quick feels Fish beneath him, trying to come up. Lester lifts Quick off but he can't see anything. By the time they get the net off Fish and get him to the shore he is dead, but Oriel refuses to accept this and she brings him back by beating on his chest and crying out to Jesus. Reluctantly, Fish comes back, screaming and spouting water from his mouth into Oriel's face.

When Fish revives, the family declare that it is a miracle, but Quick realises that 'not all of Fish Lamb had come back.' (p32)

III

We go back in time to learn the history of a large house in the city. Its owner is a rich and lonely woman who is talked (by the local priest) into taking in 'native' (Aboriginal) young women. She sets about trying to teach them to be 'ladies'. The young women are miserable and one night, one of them suicides by drinking ant poison. The woman evicts all the others and burns the linen from their beds. Two weeks later she drops dead at the piano, her nose hitting middle C.

The house is bought by lucky cousin Joel, who intends to retire to it one day. When he dies he leaves it and two thousand pounds to his cousin Sam Pickles. The house is Number One Cloud Street, in Perth.

The Pickles move up to the city, to Cloud Street. Rose smells 'meat' in a room that contains a piano, and chooses another room (an *Anne of Green Gables* room) for herself. Sam declares that they are rich, but they seem lost in such a big house. Dolly is restless and Rose looks out of her window at the world.

The Lambs are on the move. We sense that they are fleeing the country, that the Fish 'miracle' has turned sour and that Fish is at once with them and not. They answer an ad for accommodation in the city (Perth) and arrive at No 1 Cloud Street after dark. Lester meets Sam, noticing his missing fingers and recognising grief in his face. When Sam asks if they are Catholic, Lester says: 'No, nothing' indicating that they have lost their faith.

They divide the house in two and set up living together. Each family looks down on the other and they do not speak. Ted and Chub refer to Fish as a 'slowbo', something akin to the contemporary term 'retard'. Rose sees him later on the landing staring at the stars – 'His eyes were black. He was beautiful.' (p 51)

References to 'the war' place the story in the early to mid 1940s.

In 'The Knife Never Lies', Lester spins the knife as he and the kids wait for dinner. The knife decides, for example, 'who will wash-up tonight' and 'who's got a pimple up their dimple'. But when the meal is served, Lester refuses to say Grace, saying: 'so let's not be hypocrites and thank God.' Their faith has been rocked by what has happened to Fish.

Lester comes up with the idea of turning the front room of the house into a 'corner shop'. Oriel has to admit that it's a good idea, although she knows who will have to make it work. Oriel thinks about her life and finds it easier to believe in chance as the determiner of things in the world (not God).

Oriel opens the shop and it is a success. Dolly resents it. The Lambs become known in the district as 'the boxy woman' or 'sergeant-major' and 'that daft beanpole husband of hers.' Oriel gives the orders and Lester does the baking. People refer to the shop as 'Cloudstreet', one word.

We find that Quick is feeling guilty about what happened to Fish. Also, Oriel tells Lester that she blames Quick and Lester and God for what happened. Oriel and Lester take Fish to the doctor. Fish is able to recognise and name Lester, but not Oriel. The doctor says that he is 'traumatised'. He asks Fish: 'where do you want to go?' and Fish replies: 'The water, the water!' On p 69 the narrator describes Fish as 'stuck somewhere' and 'half in and half out.'

One afternoon, a 'blackfella' turns up at the door selling stick 'props'. Lester invites him in but he runs off, leaving the props, which Oriel then uses to prop up her clothes-line.

The war ends and there is an impromptu celebration that brings the Lambs and Pickles together. Even Rose goes down stairs and joins in.

IV

Sam goes off gambling, playing two-up. He returns a couple of days later, saying that he has won a job. He backs a horse called Blackbutt and it wins a few weeks in a row.

Quick sees a poor schoolboy called Wagga McBride get killed by a passing train. He becomes depressed. Lester tells him that the family owes Fish for his being 'busted in the head.' 'We were stupid enough to drown him trying to save him.' (p 94) Quick finds that, like the others, he cannot pray.

We learn that Oriel's father was like Lester – well intentioned but never quite up to anything. Oriel's mother and sisters perished in a fire and Oriel had to nurse her father's through his grief. The implication is that no-one helped Oriel with her grief.

Sam talks Lester into going to the races, and they both win. Next day Lester takes the family on a trip to Fremantle and buys a boat. It won't fit on the back of the truck, so Lester suggests that Quick row it home and Quick asks that he take Fish with him. Throughout all this, Oriel becomes increasingly agitated, but she says nothing. Later, Quick wonders whether he can do it. Back at home, as darkness approaches, things become more and more tense. Lester takes off in the truck to try to find them. At dawn he finds them asleep in the boat, ashore at Nedlands. At 9am they arrive at home, pushing the truck which has run out of petrol. Oriel is livid with Lester as she holds the boys to her. She feels that they are foreigners – 'her blood but lost to her.' (p116)

The Pickles join the Lamb's Guy Fawkes' night bonfire and potatoes. Quick thinks that Rose is in love with Fish.

One day, Lester comes upon Fish having a conversation with the pig. Lester tells Oriel: 'It talks in tongues'.

On New Years Day 1949, Oriel moves her things out of the house and into a tent pitched under the mulberry tree. The house, the pig, Fish not acknowledging her – these things are weighing on her. She feels that the house is telling her to wait.

V

Quick and Rose are sixteen. He punishes himself over Fish by surrounding himself with images of human misery and evil. He notices that Rose is getting thinner. When she eats, she throws up. One afternoon, scared by the sounds coming from the piano in the house, Quick runs down the stairs with a duffle bag over his shoulder. He accidentally hits Rose in the face and she goes out cold. Quick bolts. Oriel administers first aid to Rose.

Everyone, especially Fish, misses Quick. Lester wonders what he did wrong to turn Quick away. A rival shop opens, run by a G. (Gerry) M. Clay of the AIF. Oriel takes him on and wipes his business out of existence. In the meantime, Gerry Clay becomes Dolly's lover.

Tensions are rising in the Pickles family. Rose is in love with Fish, she watches as he plays the piano. Sam confronts her about not eating. Dolly tells her she will have to leave school and get a job, because they can't manage. Rose points out that this is because Dolly drinks and Sam gambles. Dolly threatens to strike Rose and Sam threatens to throw Dolly out 'on the street where you fuckin belong'.

Fish tells Lester that he wants to go in the boat with Quick and 'I want the water, Lestah.' (p 165) He also says that the house is sad and he knows because it talks.

Sam, in the bathroom, contemplates suicide. Rose enters and interrupts him. They talk about luck and determining one's own destiny. Rose promises herself that she will get out of this house/ family one day.

Oriel goes to the Clays to offer them a job working for the Lambs and Mrs Clay tells her to go away. Oriel has a strong sense of guilt and she accounts for her brutal fighting of the 'war' against the Clays as a reaction to her 'loss' of her two sons (Fish and Quick). She realises that this must be how Sam feels, having lost his fingers. She weeps. Rose sees her crying 'like a person'. Dolly comes home with one side of her face bruised and bleeding – a 'parting gift' from Gerry Clay. Rose tells her: 'Hating you is the best part of bein alive!' (p 175) Soon after, Rose gets a job in the city as a switch-girl.

The Lambs close the shop for a couple of days and head for the river to catch crabs. Oriel contemplates the significance of rivers in her life. She remembers being baptised, meeting Lester and losing Fish in or near rivers. At night, Oriel ties Fish to a tree to prevent him from running to the water. The narrator, Fish's other self, assures him that his time will come.

Hattie gets a boyfriend. Rose starts to eat again. Oriel considers her life as hell. She hates being a survivor. Ted Pickles leaves home. A stranger comes around claiming that his daughter is pregnant to Ted. The Lambs get a postcard from Quick, saying he's OK. The house sighs, but only Fish listens. Lester tells Fish a story from his childhood, but Fish interprets it as a story about himself, going to 'heaven' in the water.

VI

A young man is sleeping in a ute. He wakes and talks to his dog, Bill. It gradually becomes evident to the reader that this is Quick. He shoots a herd of kangaroos, using the ute's battery to run a spotlight. One roo lives long enough to kick him in the chest injuring him badly. When he rouses he realises that the battery is dead and he must walk to safety. He hallucinates, seeing Fish before him rowing in a box that says 'Harvey Oranges'. A landowner, 'Old Wentworth' finds him unconscious out in the open and saves him. Later, Lucy, Old Wentworth's daughter, gives Quick his first sexual experience by 'slipping her grabbers into his boxers.' (p 202)

It gets around that Quick is the best shot in the district, so five cockies (landowners) sign him to protect their crops from kangaroos. One night he has a vision of himself running at the spotlight. After that he regularly sees himself amongst the prey. He wonders if he is 'orright' (sane). He and Lucy meet regularly until they are caught in an apparently compromising situation and Quick has to leave town.

As he drives outside Bruce Rock, he picks up an aboriginal hitch-hiker. He tells him his story. The black man directs Quick back to the city and to Cloud Street. Quick lets him out and heads off, away. He ends up in the Margaret River area, working as a driver for Lester's cousin Earl Blunt. He stays for over a year. 'He did not think of home, but home thought of him.' (p 212)

Quick remembers the 23rd Psalm as he has a near-accident in the truck. He gets a week off in Earl's boat, fixes it up and goes fishing. Miraculously, fish leap into the boat in such numbers that it sinks. Quick cannot row it to shore. He sees the black man walking on the water and laughing. On the drive back to May and Earl's, he sees both himself and the black man jumping out from behind trees. At night he dreams of being with his whole family, down by the river.

The next day, Quick is 'lit up like a sixty watt globe and he wouldn't stop crying.' (p 219) Earl and May decide to take him home to Cloudstreet.

VII

Everyone is up early to prepare for Hat Lamb's wedding. Suddenly Earl and May arrive, with Quick glowing in the back. Lester is plainly happy that Quick is back, while Oriel says that he could have picked a better time. Later Lester and Oriel talk about beliefs and life – Lester sees life as a struggle, whereas Oriel sees it as a war.

They celebrate Quick's return, thus rounding out the 'Prodigal Son' parallels. Quick talks to the pig and hears the house creak. He meets Beryl Lee, who Oriel has taken in.

Sam comes home beaten up by his gambling debtors. Lester helps him to escape town. One afternoon, Lester goes into the Pickles half of the house to ask Dolly how Sam is getting on. She seduces him, 'You bin waiting ten years for that.' Lester says: 'I want you not to use this against me.' (p 246)

Lester gets the money to pay off Sam's debts from the Lamb's cash savings, but Sam insists on 'investing' it at a two-up game. Lester can't believe the situation he has got himself into. He tells Quick about it and about a recurrent dream he has – being carried to safety by his father during a flood. When Quick leaves, Beryl comes in and tells Lester to 'leave off with Mrs Pickles.' (p 259)

Both Oriel and Red notice that Beryl is 'fadin'. Beryl goes to Lester again and confesses that she is in love with him and has decided to join a convent – a marriage of a different kind.

Oriel asks Quick to accompany her prawning. Quick says it's silly as it's the wrong season, and Oriel says: 'Everyone else can be silly all day long in this house, so why not me a couple of hours in my lifetime?' (p 266) It is the first time she has been prawning since Fish nearly drowned. When she gets him alone, Oriel quizzes Quick about his feelings about Fish: 'You think it should have been you.' (p 268) Oriel sees both herself and Quick as guilt-ridden survivors. Eventually Quick relaxes enough to tell her she's bossy, to which Oriel merely laughs. Suddenly and impossibly, they are inundated with prawns. The net isn't big enough so they have to remove their clothes and tie them up as prawn bags.

Sam wins at two-up – 'the prince of losers, winning the bank.' (p 272) So both families have a sense of plenty. Lester invites the Pickles over for prawns. Upstairs, Fish talks to 'the shadow girl', a ghost who disappears when Quick comes.

VIII

Rose is twenty-four years old. She meets Toby Raven, a university educated journalist. On their first date she feels uncomfortable because of the educational/social difference between them (and his bad driving) but she goes along with it and loses her virginity in his flat. 'By the time summer came, Rose knew she was in love.' (p 290) Rose adapts to Toby's circle of friends but still feels uncomfortable. She types his poems, then declares that she's not a typist and he's not a poet.

One afternoon Toby shows up at Cloudstreet, announcing that someone is publishing a poem of his and that she must attend a soiree with him in the evening. It is a very posh affair indeed, but Rose does her best on the outside whilst planning her escape on the inside. It becomes apparent that the poem that these people have read and liked is not Toby's at all and that there has been some kind of mistake. In desperation, Toby tries to go along with the conversation and then tells the people about a novel he has planned about a switch-girl who used to love a slow boy and that she lives at a place where a woman lives in a tent in the backyard... He describes the whole thing as a 'grotesquerie' (a story with bizarre characters). Rose runs off, heading for the river.

At the same time, Quick comes to accept that Cloudstreet has some kind of hold on him. He repairs the boat that he and Fish had rowed back from Fremantle all those years ago. He takes up fishing and does well enough to supply the shop with the fish it needs. Sometimes Lester goes out with him. Out on the river, Lester and Quick talk about ambitions and the value of the family. Fish wants to go as well and he reminds Quick of the night 'We goed in the stars' (p 301) but Quick tells him that Oriel doesn't want Fish on the river.

One afternoon, Quick gives in to Fish and takes him along. Out on the river they hear crying. It is...Rose Pickles! She says: 'Quick Lamb...That bloody house won't leave us alone, will it?' (p 307) Fish, with his otherworldly understanding, is 'smiling fit to sin.' Fish proceeds to go to sleep as, after living in the same house for fifteen years, Quick and Rose get to know one another. After a while she even asks: 'You reckon we'd be any good married to each other?'

Rose helps with the fishing, then they go back to Cloudstreet and make love in the library, watched open-mouthed by the ghosts. In the morning they tell their respective parents that they are getting married.

Six weeks later, they are married in a church, with Fish as best man. As Rose shuffles down the aisle, Fish begins to sing or speak in tongues and rattle the box with the rings in it for percussion. This goes on for an uncomfortable length of time but eventually he lies down and sleeps. The reception is at the local RSL. Towards the end of it, in a gesture of unity and good-will, Oriel gets Dolly up and they dance together.

'They look so bloody dignified, says Rose. So proud. As they wheel by like a miracle, there are spectators weeping.' (p 321)

It is worth noting, that in early drafts, the novel ended here.

IX

Rose and Quick go crabbing on their honeymoon. On the way back, Rose announces that she wants to buy a new house to live in – 'that only *we* live in, Quick.' (p 326) Quick says he will join the police force: 'I want to fight evil.' They rent a flat while the house is being built, Rose works and Quick does police training. There is some conflict brewing between Rose and Oriel, in terms of who is the boss, who 'owns' Quick and whether Rose is permitted to call her 'Oriel'. Quick finishes his police training and Rose announces that she is pregnant.

Sam wakes up with his stump tingling and the sense of the shifty shadow about him. Dolly falls down the stairs and breaks her leg. Oriel, preparing for the day, looks at the names of the family Lamb, written on the inside cover of her Bible. Ted, in Adelaide, has a heart attack in a sauna and dies. Fish plays the piano, but all that comes out is the drone of middle C. When Quick gets home from work, Rose is having a miscarriage and she loses the baby.

Grieving her brother and her baby, Rose stops eating again. She quits her job as she is 'too weak and spiritless to get through the day anymore.' (p 339) Quick misses Cloudstreet. He misses the sounds and the life of it – he can't imagine he and Rose living in the new place they are building.

Sam gambles away his wages and Dolly pawns their possessions for drink. One morning Sam hears a thumping noise in the library. When he gets there he sees one of the ghosts and a naked Fish yelling at her to allow him to play. He thinks he has seen that old hag Lady Luck. Elaine comes to help him with Fish.

Dolly goes missing. Sam appeals to Rose to help him look for her, but she refuses. Rose remembers the afternoon when Sam lost his fingers and she found her mother in bed with a stranger. She thinks that she turned to 'steel' that afternoon. Quick arrives and whisks her off to the Cloudstreet in a taxi. 'We've found your Mum.' (p 350) Rose talks briefly to Dolly who begs her to come back the next day and Lester advises her to as well. Next day Dolly tells Rose about her background, that Dolly's mother was her sister, that Dolly is the product of incest. Dolly and Rose weep together.

Things brighten, Rose takes up swimming and falls pregnant again. The new house is nearly ready, but the black man appears to Quick again, telling him that this is not Quick's real home.

Lon gets a girl named Pansy Mullet pregnant and Oriel insists that he marry her.

The Nedlands Monster begins his murder spree. Quick thinks it is evil at work. Rose and Quick move back to Cloudstreet so that she'll have company and protection while he's at work. She notices how happy Quick is to be back and she gradually admits that she is too.

The Nedlands Monster murders and rapes a young woman. The whole city is gripped in outrage and fear, but Oriel continues to sleep unprotected in the tent. Quick considers a transfer to the 'traffic police', but the fact that the Monster keeps striking and evading them is making him depressed. Fish hears him crying in the toilet.

On the night the news comes that they have caught the Monster, Quick gets a call to go home as Rose is in labour. The Monster is a pathetic figure, father of seven with a hare lip. Rose gives birth to Harry at Cloudstreet, everybody present and proceedings presided over by Oriel. Quick says he looks waxy, so Lester dubs him 'Wax Harry'. Harry's birth purges the house of its history of suffering – 'the house breaths its first painless breath in half a century' and the pig squeals 'like the voice of God'. (p 385).

X

Everybody loves Wax Harry – Dolly brings her friends over to see him, Sam sneaks him peppermints and Oriel lets Rose help in the shop. Elaine tells Rose that she is just like a young Oriel and Rose chokes.

Lon and Pansy's child is born – a daughter called Merileen-Gaye.

United States President John Kennedy is assassinated and the Nedlands Monster is sentenced to death. When Quick expresses satisfaction at the latter, Lester says 'He's only a man'. (p 395) Oriel calls the death sentence 'Barbarism!' and becomes quite upset, leaving the room. Lester reads to Quick and Rose from the Bible (p 395). The passage says that Jesus said that the two greatest commandments are that you love God and love your neighbour. Quick says that since Fish, Oriel can't believe these things. Lester says that Oriel works at trying to believe them. Then Lester is also overcome by emotion and leaves. Quick is surprised at their reaction. Lester secretly goes to a (Catholic) church on Sunday.

Quick is transferred to 'traffic' and he likes it and relaxes. Until one afternoon as he eats his lunch by the river he sees that two kids have found a floating body. He jumps in and pulls the body in – it is a child and long dead. When he gets it to shore he cannot look its face because it reminds him of Harry and himself as a kid and Fish. Later he is told that the child is the son of the Nedlands Monster. This forces him to understand what Lester had said, that the Monster is just a man.

Pansy is pregnant again. Lon takes the day off work so Oriel forces him to help out by loading the truck. In anger, he does a sloppy job so Oriel puts him over her knee and spanks him with a wooden plank. In front of the crowd that has gathered, Lon breaks away saying: 'Carn, then put yer dukes up woman!' (p 401) Oriel does and KO's him with a left. She then turns on the crowd and insists that they help reload the truck in return for the entertainment. They do.

The black man appears to Sam, telling him not to sell Cloudstreet and have it knocked down for flats. Next day Dolly also tells Sam not to sell.

Quick and Rose decide to go on a holiday before they move to the new house. The evening before, Oriel invites everyone to dinner in Lester's room. After dinner, Oriel asks Sam about his intentions to sell, saying 'This place has been good to me.' Dolly says 'The bloody place has got to us.' (p 411) Sam declares 'We stay.' Everyone sings the national anthem, with Lester on the accordion, to celebrate.

Fish begs Quick to take him on the holiday too, and Rose insists he come. On the first day Fish and Harry both need 'changing', Quick gets Fish and Rose gets Harry. That evening Rose tells Quick that she doesn't want to leave Cloudstreet. 'We belong to it...It's a bloody tribe, a new tribe.' Quick confesses that he has felt the same for months.

During the night, Quick wakes to see a moonlike glow coming off Fish. Then they all watch as an endless stream of naked children seem to rise out of the ground and part the wheat, moving around and past them all night.

The narrator Fish addresses the physical Fish, saying 'soon you'll be yourself and we'll be us; you and me.' (p 420)

Quick and Rose return to Cloudstreet with the news that they are staying. Lester proposes a picnic and Oriel says to lock the shop and 'Let's do it right for once!'

Down at the river, everything is laid out. Everybody joins in 'a mad, yokel twenty year-dance'. The 'missing' have also turned up. And one is 'going' – Fish.

The world goes on. The Nedlands Monster is hung and denied his last wish to be buried with his drowned son.

The black man leaves 'the trees like a bird and goes laughing into the sun'.

Fish heads for the water. Quick sees him and runs towards him, shouting alarm. But then he stops himself, and starts to cry. Fish returns to the water, drowning, to be reunited with his other self. 'Being Fish Lamb. Perfectly. Always. Everyplace. Me.' (p 424)

Epilogue

Two unnamed women ('the little boxy' and 'the big blowsy') dismantle a tent in a backyard that yesterday had had a fence dividing it. They fold it and carry it into the house.

Oriel is returning to Cloudstreet with the assistance of Dolly. So the resolution has been effected and the Lambs and Pickles are united.

SETTING

Setting is a factor in all novels, but it is especially important in *Cloudstreet*. Remember that Winton once described his characters as 'figures in landscape', suggesting that place is the most important thing to him about characterisation.

The novel is about 'place' – about the efficacious nature of being where you belong.

Both the Pickles and the Lambs begin the novel living in the country. Sam is an itinerant worker and the Lambs have been unsuccessfully working the land. Both families come to the city Perth because they have no real options. The Lambs are fleeing from the misery of their loss of faith after Fish's partial resurrection. Later, when Quick runs away, he runs to the country and seems to feel comfortable there. But Rose does the opposite – her 'prodigal' period is deep in the city, the sophisticated and educated city. So, the novel does not present us with a simple 'rural' vs 'city' paradigm.

Perth

The novel shows Perth in its infancy, reflecting the fact that Australia is a nation in its infancy. There is a sense of potential and incompleteness. It is civilised to some extent, but it still can be a wild place, where a situation like the Nedlands Monster can flourish.

The river dominates the city and is enfolded by it. The river (natural) and the city (man made) co-exist.

The River

The river is a very important setting in the novel. At one point, Oriel considers how often rivers have been a part of her life.

The most significant events on a river in the book are, of course, Fish's near drowning and then his actual drowning at the end. The water is Fish's 'place', it is his home where he can achieve wholeness and peace. You might consider that his destiny was originally to drown at nine years old, on the night of the prawning accident, but Oriel intervenes.

There is peace on the river on other occasions in the novel. Quick and Fish's trip in the boat from Fremantle to (as it turns out) Nedlands, although it is a stupid and reckless concept, is a time of peace under the stars and on the water for Fish especially. As well, Quick finds peace on the river during his fishing expeditions after he has returned from Earl's. And Rose seeks solace on the river after leaving the literary soiree she is attending with Toby Raven. She seeks solace and she finds love and destiny.

On two occasions, the river yields up plenitude in the form of fish and prawns.

There is a sense in all of these instances that the river is a natural environment unspoiled by human interference. That the natural world is benevolent and will provide. It is to the river that the Lambs and Pickles go, united in the birth of Wax Harry. This provides the scene of glorious good-hearted celebration that gives Fish his opportunity to leave once and for all.

The House

The house is a place, an environment and a personality. Cloudstreet, one word as it becomes known in the district, is a place that is at first unsettled and troubled. But by the end it is purged of all this and ready to receive Oriel back into its domain.

Both Quick and Rose try (twice) to leave Cloudstreet and both of them are forced back before they realise that it is where they belong. Cloudstreet is the 'place' of everyone in the novel except Fish.

Cloud is a natural image and street is a man made image. It also combines the ethereal and the mundane. So, Cloudstreet is a place where opposites are reconciled. Think of Dolly and Oriel. The living and the dead.

Historical Context

The other aspect of setting is 'When' a story takes place. *Cloudstreet* is rooted firmly in the 1940s to early 1960s. This is established through reference to historical events such as World War II, the assassination of President Kennedy of the USA and the Nedlands Monster.

More important than the historical events, *Cloudstreet* is clearly a product of nostalgia for this era. The colloquialisms, such as 'chiaking' and 'skylarking' (p 1) are drawn from the Australia of that era. The values and the way of life are a long way off the Australia of today. The novel, for example, contains no reference to television!

It is often said that *Cloudstreet* is a very 'Australian' novel. The characters and the language are particularly Australian in character – or, at least, the way Australians still see themselves. In truth, though, the novel is very much representative of Australia in the middle of the twentieth century. Winton wrote the novel in the late 1980s/early 90s and there is a strong sense of nostalgia for an Australia gone. The novel is an homage to an Australia that has passed.

CHARACTER ANALYSIS

Winton's writing is most prized for its characters, which somehow succeed in being larger than life and realistic at the same time. *Cloudstreet* is peopled with the most bizarre and somehow likeable group of characters.

Fish Lamb

Christened Samson Lamb, Fish (short for Samson-fish) is the most well-loved child in town, favourite of his mother Oriel. At nine years old he nearly drowns in a prawning accident which leaves both his father and his big brother Quick riddled with guilt. Dead, he is dragged onto the shore and revived by the sheer will power of his mother, who beats him on the chest as she cries out to God that he be saved.

When he revives, the family proclaims a genuine family miracle, but Quick is the first to understand that 'not all of Fish Lamb had come back'. Thereafter, Fish is mentally disabled, a child caught in an ever more adult body. He cannot look after himself. Also, he craves the water and death.

Fish has a kind of 'idiot savant' quality which enables him to tune into the ghosts in the library at Cloudstreet and to hold conversations with the pig. He has an insight into things that is extraordinary but it is impossible for him to express it to others.

Fish is also separate and otherworldly and it is this which causes Rose Pickles to fall in love with him for a time. But the other Pickles call him a 'slowbo', the 1940s equivalent of a 'retard'.

Fish is affectionate to everyone in the family, especially Quick, except that from the time of the 'accident' he is unable to recognise Oriel. It is as though he holds her responsible for his current torturous situation of being half with the living and half in the spirit world. His only real desire is to reintegrate with his other self by going back to the water and drowning. This is what he does on page 424, but only after everything is settled in the house and with the two families.

Fish is the central character of the novel as what the novel has to say about human existence is captured most in Fish's story. Winton's representation of Fish's death is fascinating because it is a triumphant release from the misery of his situation into a fantastic state of unity with himself and with the universe. It shows existence as continuous, as real on a physical and spiritual level.

As well, it is an unusually positive representation of death. At the end of the Prologue, we are asked to worry, not about the dying, but about the living 'who go on down the close, foetid galleries of time and space without you.' (p 3) In 'Moon Sun Stars', Fish's death is a reunification and a liberation. It is what he has craved since Oriel dragged him back on the river bank. In that scene as well, it is the return to life that is agony for Fish.

Fish is also the **narrator** of the novel. *Cloudstreet* is Fish telling us his story in the moment of his dying – 'as long as it took to tell you all this.' (p 424) Also, in the Prologue: 'having known the story for just a moment.'

There are a few sections of the novel where Fish the narrator addresses Fish the character, for example 'Soon' on page 420, when the spirit Fish reassures the physical Fish that they will be together soon: 'soon you'll be yourself, and we'll be us; you and me. Soon!' Another example is 'Coming' on page 403: 'You're coming to me Fish...The house is clear, the people are coming to things day by day and it's all that's left...Your turn is coming.'

In these sections, Winton makes it more explicit that one Fish (the dead or spiritual Fish, the part that *didn't* come back) is narrating the story from a position of knowledge and understanding 'on the other side'. The physical Fish has no knowledge or real understanding, though he is tuned into the supernatural things around him – the house, the pig and the ghosts. More than anything, he has a powerful desire to return to the water and reunite with his other self.

Quick Lamb

Christened Mason Lamb, Quick is called 'Quick' because he isn't. He is a cautious and deliberate person. At eleven years old, out prawning with his father and brother Fish, he becomes aware that Fish has gone under the net and is trapped. As best he can, he helps his father drag Fish in to shore, but they both know that Fish is dead. When his mother revives Fish and the family claims a miracle, he knows that all is not right. Thereafter he carries a burden of guilt over what has happened to his brother.

This makes him predisposed to look on the gloomier pessimistic aspects of life. As a teenager, he decorates the walls of his room at Cloudstreet with pictures and stories that demonstrate the misery of human life. He witnesses a fellow student at school, Wogga MacBride, get killed by a passing train. When this sense of gloom and guilt overwhelms him, he packs a knapsack (accidentally hitting Rose in the face with it as he heads down the stairs) and bolts.

This following phase of Quick's life parallels the story of the Prodigal Son in the Bible, in the sense that he leaves, has some experiences in the outside world and then returns.

Quick makes a living by culling kangaroos for rich landowners. He also has his first romance with a girl called Lucy Wentworth, the daughter of one of these landowners. When they are caught one night in an apparently compromising situation, Quick has to leave town, well...quickly.

He picks up a black man and gives him a lift back to the city. The black man, in fact, directs Quick back home to Cloudstreet, but Quick resists and drives off. He ends up working for Lester's cousin Earl.

During his time away, Quick encounters a number of supernatural or psychic experiences. When he is injured by the kangaroo, he hallucinates that he sees Fish rowing in a box which says 'Harvey Oranges'. This vision relates back to when they were children and Lester asked them to row home in the boat that he had bought because he couldn't fit it in the truck. For Quick, it is a memory of contentment, out on the river with Fish under the stars. The fact that Fish is rowing an oranges box in mid air makes the vision comical as well as optimistic. It is as though Fish has come to save him in a manner that only Fish would feel confident about.

After he recovers and meets Lucy, Quick gets lots of work as a marksman culling kangaroos. But he starts to see himself amongst the kangaroo herds, in the spotlight and in the sights of his gun. This image is one of a fear of self-destruction. It is as though Quick is being told that he is in danger of killing himself as well as the kangaroos. This could mean that Quick is not a natural killer and that he loves the wildlife and the environment. It could also relate to Quick's as yet unrecognised need to return home to Cloudstreet. It is as though he is killing his true self by staying away.

Fish is led back home by the black man but he resists and takes up working with Earl. A year goes by then he takes a week off and goes fishing. Out on the Margaret River, fish come to him like a miracle, they hurl themselves onto the boat – so many of them that he can't row the boat back into shore. This is an image of plenitude. It symbolises the bounty and generosity of nature and perhaps God, if you want to see it in that way. The world will provide. Life is generous. It is also a Christian image. The apostles of Jesus were fishermen and they had caught nothing one afternoon. Jesus told them to cast their nets over the other side and the nets were filled with fish. Quick is being called back to the fold, to Cloudstreet and the family. He isn't meant to be alone.

Also, he is meant to be a fisherman. So that he can be out on the river fishing and catching the biggest fish he catches – Rose.

Soon after this, Quick sees the black man walking on the water, as Jesus had done, reported in the book of Luke. This suggests that the black man is always with him and that he intends to save him in some way or another. The fact that he is laughing suggests that he's telling Quick that there is no point in resisting and that things will go as they are meant to in the long run.

When Quick returns to the house of Earl and May, he starts having his old visions of human suffering, but then he dreams of the family. He wakes up glowing – 'lit up like a sixty-watt globe'. Upon seeing this, Earl and May decide to take him home, and they do.

What is meant by Quick glowing? All I can suggest is that it is a final danger signal for his well-being and self. It is like when the temperature gauge on your car lights up or goes into the red. You have to stop, or you'll wreck your engine. After a couple of days back at Cloudstreet, Quick stops glowing and returns to his normal self.

Quick learns a lot about life and some things about himself, during his time away, but it is vital and inevitable that he return. Like the Prodigal Son in the Bible, Quick has to sink to his lowest before returning. As in the Bible, his return is celebrated by the family.

One big difference is that in the Bible story, the brothers of the Prodigal are jealous of the father's happiness when he returns and point out that while the Prodigal has been gallivanting around, they have been the ones who have worked the family property and kept things going. They are the ones that deserve the father's love, not the Prodigal. By contrast, the Lamb's joy at Quick's return is uncomplicated. Jealousy doesn't seem to occur to any of them, ever. They are Lambs.

One way of looking at the Prodigal Son section of the novel is to point out the contrast that Quick comes back, where Fish did not. This is especially true for Oriel, whom Fish can't even recognise.

Quick repairs the old boat that he and Fish had tried to row home and takes up fishing for the family shop. One evening he gives in to Fish's requests and takes him with him onto the river, so that they miraculously bump into Rose who has gone to the river to rid herself of Toby Raven. She is at the end of her own 'prodigal' period, where she has left her family socially rather than physically.

While the union of Rose and Quick could be described as glaringly predictable, that is part of Winton's point. Though both of them have tried to go off in vastly different directions, neither can escape their destiny. Life has brought them back to each other and will lead them back to Cloudstreet in the end. Life knew where they belonged even if they didn't. It is appropriate that Fish is on hand to witness the event as he has been the connection between them – they have both been fixated on him in the past for different reasons – Quick because of his guilt and Rose because to her Fish was beautiful and other-worldly.

Marrying Rose and joining the police force looks like suburban conformity for Quick, but he has some more lessons to learn yet. He watches in horror as Rose miscarries their first child, unable to do anything to save her from this.

The case of the Nedlands Monster has a profound effect on Quick. He had told Rose that he was joining the police force in order to fight evil, and he sees the Nedlands Monster as pure evil. It makes him miserable that the Monster continues to defy police attempts to identify and catch him. Rose even moves back to Cloudstreet in order to be safe while Quick is at work. When the Monster is caught and tried, Quick applauds the death sentence being applied. Then one day he is having lunch beside the river and he sees a body floating on the water. He tries to rescue the boy but he is already dead. Quick sees Harry's face, his own face and Fish's face in the face of the drowned. Later Quick finds out that the boy is the son of the Nedlands Monster. Quick understands that the Monster is just a man with a family and now a dead son. 'The poor bastard, he thought' and later he tells Rose 'But it's not us and them anymore. It's us and us and us. It's always us...But there's no monsters, only people like us.'

He comes to understand that even the Nedlands Monster is a man like him or anyone else.

Quick and Rose are good enough to take Fish with them when they and Harry go on a road trip. Quick even has to clean Fish's bum after he 'soils himself' in his pants. But they are rewarded with a supernatural experience as hoards of children move across the fields in the middle of the night. It is an image of unity and home.

This experience prepares for their decision to stay at Cloudstreet rather than move to their recently completed house. This decision completes the 'Prodigal' cycles, as they now go home together forever. By doing this, they create the circumstances in which Fish can return to the water and his other self.

Quick has one last great action in the novel and that is to not take action as he sees his brother heading for the water where he will drown. In this final moment, Quick has the wisdom and love to let Fish go.

The lessons that Quick learns in the novel are intended to inform the reader as well. If Fish is the central character in terms the novel's ideas about existence, it is Quick who dominates the narrative.

Quick's function in the novel is as a common likeable person to whom the reader can relate. Like Rose, he sits in the middle of his family's trials and troubles and the reader sympathises with him. The reader sees him as being hard on himself by wanting to accept the blame for Fish's predicament. We understand his desire to get out but are pleased when he comes back. If the novel has a hero it is Quick in his shambling common-man way. His final act of heroism is when he lets Fish go back to the water.

Rose Pickles

Rose is, from the novel's outset, both outside of the Pickles family and its great hope. Although she craves a life away from her family, in the end by following her heart, she saves them. Dolly, Sam and Chubb are gathered up in the combined Lamb/Pickles family that settles into life in Cloudstreet at the end of the novel. This is because of Rose and her gift of Wax Harry.

The narrative opens with the day that ruins Sam and becomes Rose's trauma – her father has lost the fingers of one hand in a work accident and she must find her mother to let her know. She goes to the room in the pub in which the family lives and finds her mother having sex with a stranger. In her own terms, this turns Rose into 'steel'. She closes off her emotions and makes herself invulnerable.

She is standoffish and superior in her dealings with the Lambs, except for the fact that she is attracted to Fish. Fish is also alone in a way, and he seems otherworldly. He sees and hears things that others don't.

As an adolescent, Rose suffers an eating disorder that is something in the nature of bulimia – she purges by throwing up whatever she eats. This condition appears to come from her need to feel that she can control something in her own life with her family disintegrating around her. She is the strong one, by comparison.

She leaves school in order to get a job that might support the family, as Dolly drinks so much and Sam gambles. She gets a job as a receptionist and settles into life in the city. She even eats and puts on some weight. She meets Toby Raven through her job and soon she is having her first romance with him. He is a journalist with aspirations as a poet and dramatist.

Rose attends a literary soiree with him to celebrate the fact that one of his poems is to be published. It turns out to be a case of mistaken identity, but Toby regales the literary types around him with the plan he has for a novel based on Rose's family and living circumstances. He represents Rose's situation as an amusing 'grotesquerie' (exaggerated and bizarre characters). Naturally enough, Rose is offended and runs off, heading for the solace of the river. It is here that she encounters Quick and Fish, and Quick and Rose fall in love.

As a married woman, she sets about establishing the goal that she and Quick have their own place. She has suburban dreams of a house and a lawn, all neat and tidy. They rent a flat and start to build. It is fair to say that the reader does not take these intentions all that seriously as a potential road to happiness for Rose, but we can understand how her life so far with the Pickles has given her the impression that hum-drum suburban security would be preferable.

Rose loses her first baby at the same time as Dolly loses her favourite one – Ted. Rose fights off resentment, jealousy and depression and stops eating again. Eventually she is pregnant again and the threat of the Nedlands Monster draws her back to Cloudstreet.

In the Biblical pattern of the novel, Rose is Mary, as she gives birth to the child who saves the two families by uniting them. Rose is the mother/agent of unity. Wax Harry is the embodiment of it.

On page 391, Elaine points out that Rose is just like a young Oriel. Rose doesn't take too kindly to this suggestion ('Rose choked.' p 392), but it is a perspective that may well have occurred to the reader at least a hundred pages earlier. They are both survivors of family dysfunction and have both had to be more mature than their years at an early age. They both played the steady reliable role in families that had come apart. Consequently, they are both independent minded and inclined to be bossy. As well, the narrator Fish uses Rose's word 'steel' (p 336) in advising Oriel that she must wait and be strong. (p 397) Not long after Rose and Quick's marriage, there are suggestions that we are headed for conflict between the two, for example there are issues over who 'owns' Quick and Oriel resents Rose calling her 'Oriel', but Winton never really pursues these. All conflict is lost in the birth of Harry and Fish's return to the water. It is, perhaps, interesting (even surprising) that Rose plays no part in the Epilogue's symbolic gestures of unity as Oriel comes back into the house. I guess you would need to ask Tim Winton about that one!

In the end, she is as happy as Quick to return to Cloudstreet permanently. She understands that this is her true place.

Rose's function in the novel is to parallel Quick as the Pickle's 'Prodigal Daughter'. Through her association with Toby Raven, she 'leaves' the Pickles' social level and moves into a more (apparently) sophisticated and pretentious world of education and art. She is never quite comfortable, but she does succeed in entering that world and, in the end, it is important that she rejects it rather than vice versa. Even though she has always been the severest critic of her mother and father, she is not going to tolerate having them run down and made fun of by Toby in an attempt to win some laughs and kudos from people who don't even know who he is.

As with Quick, the reader sympathises with Rose's situation – having a gambling father and a drinking promiscuous mother.

Rose is the hope of the Pickles and the agent of their salvation through Harry and unification with the Lambs.

Oriel Lamb

When Fish drowns in the prawning accident, Oriel refuses to let him go. She beats on his chest and calls out to Jesus to bring him back. Winton recounts this scene mostly from Fish's point of view: 'Worse, he's slipping back and the gash in the grey recedes and darkness returns and pain and the most awful sickening feeling in him...' The return to life is a painful horrid experience. Thus Oriel bringing Fish back to life is depicted as a victory of her will over Fish's. This strength of will is characteristic of Oriel. It is her power but she is also punished for it.

Thereafter, Fish is unable to recognise his own mother. And Oriel's faith in Jesus and Christianity is shaken. She blames God (and

Lester) for what has happened to Fish and for the fact that her relationship with him is destroyed.

Oriel is 'the boxy woman' and Winton often associates military imagery with her. 'We make war on the bad and don't surrender' she tells Lester, typifying her attitude to life. (p 230) In running the Cloudstreet shop, Winton refers to her as a 'quartermaster' and a 'sergeant major' and her determination to defeat and destroy the opposition shop run by GM Clay is nothing short of all-out war.

The trauma in Oriel's early life is that when she was a child her sisters and mother were killed in a bushfire that razed the farmhouse in which they lived. Oriel survives because she goes down into the cellar. Her father survives too, but greatly traumatised, to the point where 'it was *she* who nursed *him*.' (p 95) The italics in this quote reflect the fact that in normal circumstances you might rather expect the father to be strong enough to nurse the child. But not so.

This trauma is greatly added to by what happens to Fish and the effect of the false hopes raised by his 'resurrection'. Oriel says that she hates being the survivor – it is easier to be weak and be the one that falls apart or dies.

A lot of the time, Winton treats Oriel with a kind of ironic awe – we admire some of the things she achieves, but we tend to laugh at her 'behind her back'. She also comes across to us as cold, as 'steel' as she, Fish and Rose put it.

Her move to the backyard and the tent indicates an impatient rejection of the Lamb/Pickles 'nonsense' that is going on inside the house. She is also deeply hurt by Fish's failure to recognise her existence, as he was her favourite. As well, she can't take the fidgety animation of the house itself and feels that it is telling her to 'wait, wait' (as the narrator Fish also does on page 397). Oriel isn't normally one to wait: 'Everything can be helped' she tells Lester (p 230), meaning that you don't just wait for things to change, you change them yourself.

But Oriel surprises us on a couple of occasions in the novel. After his return, she insists that Quick go prawning with her, in spite of his best advice that it is out of prawning season. Oriel is showing courage in returning to a riverbank to prawn for the first time since Fish's accident. She shows a real understanding of Quick's feelings of guilt about what happened to Fish and we see the relationship between that and Oriel's own experience with her mother and sisters 'up in the house cooking like picnic steaks while she lay helpless in the cellar'. (p 268) Quick even relaxes to the point that he works up the courage to tell Oriel that she's bossy. At the end of the evening they are rewarded with an impossible catch of prawns out of season.

At Quick and Rose's wedding reception, Oriel has the sensitivity and foresight to offer Dolly a dance and lead her out in a marvellous and unlikely display of unity and peace. Only the birth of Wax Harry brings the families closer.

And Oriel does wait. Harry is born, and the house is silenced. Fish goes back to the water, and the 'little boxy woman' allows 'the big blowsy woman' to help her perform the ritual of dismantling the tent and returning to the house and the combined family.

Oriel's function in the novel is that she is the character who finds it hardest to accept things as they are. She believes that she can and should change and direct things. Her acceptance of things and return to the house consequently has a huge impact at the end.

By the way, Tim Winton's grandmother really did live in a tent!

Lester Lamb

Lester's Christian faith is also shaken by what happens to Fish but nothing shakes his faith in the family. 'There's always the family', he says to Oriel on page 232.

His spinning of the knife ('the knife never lies') is also related to his loss of faith, as it is a pagan activity.

In many ways, Lester is a wonderful example of an Australian literary and popular culture stereotype – the well-intentioned and bungling, but likeable, Dad. He is the biggest kid in the family, the least reliable, the butt of jokes behind his back – but well loved for all that.

Oriel says of him: 'He was never quite up to anything' (p 95), meaning that he has good intentions but never actually achieves anything. Apologists for Lester would probably argue that Oriel's strong tendency towards bossiness never gave him the opportunity to achieve anything on his own.

The one great thing that she has against him is that she holds him (and God) responsible for what happened to Fish. It is, to her, a great injustice that Fish talks to Lester but not to her. He also orchestrates the near-disaster of having Quick and Fish row the boat back from Fremantle together. 'Quick was starting to wonder if the old man was the full quid'. (p 112) Lester finally panics: 'Lord what a fool he was; he wasn't fit to have children, she was right.' (p 113) Luckily, he finds them at dawn on the foreshore at Nedlands.

We like Lester – he's familiar, for one thing. And most readers are likely to sympathise with the constant bucketing that he takes from Oriel, and the increasing absence of any tenderness in their relationship. I think we're supposed to forgive him his 'indiscretion' with Dolly as the action of a man who would rather have sex with his wife if he had the opportunity. Lester also rebels by going off gambling with Sam.

He also sneaks off to a Catholic church on Sundays for a time, looking for something to believe in.

Lester's great strength is his heart and his love. He displays a simple wisdom when he tells Quick to look after his 'missus' and then tells Rose not to reject her mother and be overcome by hate: 'You're one of us now and I can't bear to lose you' and 'Go on with your life, love. It's all there is.' (p 353)

Lester's function in the novel is to model a virtually unshakeable faith in the family. He provides a direct contrast, in style of parenting, to Oriel. He is also the first character to take an approach of acceptance of life, something the others all have to learn.

Oriel and Lester lamb are based on Winton's grandparents, Olive and Les Winton. The novel has aspects of biography and autobiograpy. Winton himself nearly drowned on more than one occasion. It is factual and fictive. It is Life Writing and yarn spinning, yet through all the strands of story lie a quest for unity and aspects of hope and the celebration of the strength of the human spirit. More will be said about this later. When approaching a text as part of a Critical Study, it is important to start with a close study, then analyse other opinions and interpretations and finally ensure you can justify your own opinions by rejecting and supporting those of others. look for differing approaches and interpretations but, as above, also unifying elements.

Sam Pickles

Sam believes only in luck, the luck that almost constantly deserts him. For all that, he is a compulsive gambler on a life-long losing streak.

'Sam the Slump, the bloke whose luck was running at a temporary low which began at birth and would probably stay with him to the coffin.' (p 342)

Sam has a sense of when 'the shifty shadow of God' is about and he had better watch out for what is about to happen. He has such a feeling on the day that he loses the fingers of his right hand in an industrial accident.

From that point, the right hand becomes a metaphor for Sam himself.

'She (Rose) saw the naked knuckles of his stump whitening in their hopeless effort to make a fist.' (p 168) Sam's aggression is impotent, he has no sense of purpose and feels powerless in life.

'I'm a weak, stupid, useless bastard and that's, that's...' (p 168) he says as Rose interrupts him apparently contemplating suicide. But Sam is too weak for such an act.

It is difficult for the reader to sympathise or find much to admire about Sam. He is long-suffering in the sense that his wife Dolly has many affairs. Between the two of them they demonstrate how a family should not be.

His one admirable action is to not sell Cloudstreet to developers. In this way he facilitates the two families (which by now are one) staying in the place where they belong.

Sam's function in the novel is as a demonstration of over-acceptance really. Life happens to him, he does not actively participate. His adherence to the belief in Lady Luck is a pagan empty value.

Dolly Pickles

Dolly is Sam's beautiful and promiscuous wife, mother of Rose, Ted and Chub. On the afternoon when Sam loses his fingers in the accident, she is in the room in the pub where the Pickles are staying, having sex with a stranger. Her reaction to the news about her husband is to curse that it is his right, working, hand. How will he support them?

Dolly is an irresponsible mother and a chronically unfaithful wife. She is also a drunkard. She fails to establish a relationship with Rose and treats her as a rival once she is old enough to attract men. She openly prefers Ted to her other children. She is passionate and earthy, always dreaming of being somewhere else. She mocks Sam for his weakness.

It is not until page 357 that the reader (along with Rose) gains an insight into Dolly's background and some reasons why she is the way she is. She reveals to her daughter that she grew up the victim and product of incest. Her parents were her father and her sister. Her sister was her mother and that made her father her grandfather. This is pretty much a textbook cause of the promiscuous life that Dolly has led - the confusion and substitute of sex for love.

Once Dolly has made this disclosure to Rose, their relationship flourishes and this is enhanced ten-fold by the birth of Wax Harry. Dolly dotes over him like a typical grandmother. The truth and the unity with the Lambs are Dolly's salvation.

Dolly and Oriel function in the novel as a direct juxtaposition of types of women. They are 'boxy' and 'blousey', maternal and sexual, practical and dreaming, steel and flesh. Harry's birth and Fish's death reconcile these opposites. In the end they make peace, dance together at Quick and Rose's wedding and Dolly assists in Oriel's return to the house and the unified family.

The Black Man

Readers have puzzled over the appearances of the black man, in his strange garb, throughout the novel. It has become conventional to see the black man as an angel. He is an agent of rightful destiny and his purpose seems to be to see the Pickles and Lambs to a situation where it is acceptable for Fish to return to the water. Once this is assured, his work is done and he leaves.

That Winton makes his angel an Aborigine is interesting. It is ironic, as angels are commonly depicted as blue-eyed-blonde-haired, so Winton is commenting on the xenophobia inherent in this. Also, the appearances of a black angel introduces Aboriginal culture into the novel. One of *Cloudstreet*'s main themes is 'place' – the sense of belonging in a particular landscape or to a particular house. This sense of place is a strong aspect of Aboriginal culture. In Aboriginal culture, humans belong to the land. Setting and place are equally significant in the values of *Cloudstreet*.

Following is an attempt to track the appearances of the black man in *Cloudstreet*.

The black man first appears to Lester at the door of the house. He is offering props for sale. When he enters the house he becomes highly agitated, as though he senses the supernatural disturbances therein and he runs off. Winton offers us a little link to his final appearance on page 62: 'His toes splayed on the ground like he was as much bird as he was man.'

Next he appears to Rose (p 161) apparently as a warning that she must return to life and start eating again. On page 178, the black man 'comes flying by your tree' and 'passing overhead like an owl'. The owl is associated with wisdom.

When Quick leaves the property of Lucy Wentworth's father, he picks up the black man hitch-hiking. The black man tries to direct Quick home to Cloudstreet, but Quick drops him off and bolts again. The next time Quick sees him (p 216ff) the black man walks on water like Jesus and laughs. This is immediately after Quick has caught an impossible number of fish. Then, as he drives back to Earl's, he sees alternately, himself and the black man jumping out in front of the car. Next morning Quick is glowing and the black man succeeds in shepherding him home.

When Rose and Quick try to set up house away from Cloudstreet, the black man appears (p 326 and 362) directing them back. 'This isn't your home' he tells Quick of the house they are building. When Quick finally accepts that his fate is Cloudstreet, dozens of black angels appear.

The black man appears to Sam (p 405) to make clear to him that he should not sell Cloudstreet to developers. 'You shouldn't break a place. Places are strong, important.'

When Fish heads for the water and it is clear that Quick will let him go, then the black man can go too – 'a black man leaves the trees like a bird and goes laughing into the sun.' Again, he is a bird and he leaves as his mission is completed.

A Christian reading will see the black man as a Christian angel, an agent on earth to see that God's will is done. This is one approach, although it does not take account of the fact that the angel is black. Making him black, Winton is pointing us towards Aboriginal culture with its sense of destiny and the significance of place.

Winton is saying 'Hey, look, why can't an angel be black?' And he is also saying that the significance of place in the lives of human beings as he sees it is better appreciated by Aborigines through their culture than it is by white Australians through theirs.

Ted Pickles

Ted is Dolly's favourite child and he seems to share some of her tendency towards promiscuity. Not long after he leaves home, Sam is confronted at the door by an aggrieved father claiming that Ted is the father of his daughter's coming baby. He dies of a heart attack in a sauna and Dolly's grief is so severe and dismissive of the others that it triggers an honest talk between her and Rose. This then has a very positive effect on the relationship between Dolly and Rose.

Chub Pickles

Chub seems to have inherited his father's purposelessness and his mother's tendency to imbibe – he is fat and lazy. It is a remarkable thing at the picnic at the end of the novel that 'even Chub is up off his arse and dancing' (!) It seems that he has been gathered in to the unified family like everyone else.

Hat and Elaine Lamb

Hat and Elaine are twins and the oldest of Lester and Oriel's offspring. Hat is the first of the Lambs to marry (on the very day that a glowing Quick is returned to the family by Earl and May) and after that she doesn't figure much in things. The more reserved Elaine stays on though, perpetually engaged but never married, and she is there at the end, dancing with her younger sister Red.

Red Lamb

Red is the youngest of the Lamb girls, though she is older than Quick. She is the tomboy and the most likely candidate to take over Fish's role of family joker. As a kid, she even fights boys behind the bike shed.

Lon Lamb

The youngest of the Lambs, he is married young to Pansy who is already pregnant with Merileen-Gaye, and when the novel ends she is pregnant again. Lon is a bit of a larrikin and he suffers somewhat it would seem from 'always the baby' syndrome. When he is 22 and a married father, Oriel puts him over her knee and spanks him with a fence paling for not packing the truck properly. When he challenges her to fight, she decks him with one punch. I suppose this incident tells us more about Oriel than it does about Lon!

Toby Raven

Toby is a journalist with aspirations to be a writer. He meets Rose one day over the switch-board. They meet and she falls in love with him. He introduces her to some people and an aspect of society that she would not otherwise have encountered.

The reader is always conscious of the fact that Rose is not entirely comfortable and we don't get 'inside' Toby enough to know what he sees in the relationship. It doesn't surprise us much that the relationship fails, but it does demonstrate Rose's potential as an individual.

Winton is very hard on Toby. Winton loves most of the characters in *Cloudstreet*, but not Toby. He is suspicious of him and turns him into a repugnant hypocrite at the literary soiree where he tries to impress people by making jokes at the expense of Rose and her family and the Lambs.

After all, Tim Winton has written a novel with such characters in it! The difference is that Toby refers to them as a 'grotesquerie', while Winton brings them to life like members of your own family.

In the end, Toby doesn't matter. Winton sets him up as pretentious and self-important and that's what he is.

The Nedlands Monster

The Nedlands Monster was a real historical figure named Eric Cooke. He murdered at least eight people between 1958 and 1963. He was hanged in 1964. He remains Australia's worst serial killer.

Part of Winton's purpose is to place the novel in its historical context – just as the references to World War II earlier and to the assassination of the American President John F Kennedy. His other purpose is to set up a lesson for Quick and for the reader. Quick had told Rose that he joined the police force to fight evil. To all intents and purposes, the Nedlands Monster is a clear case of pure evil, and it really hurts Quick that the police can't catch him immediately. But the experience of pulling the body of the Monster's son out of the river rams home to Quick that the Nedland's Monster is a human being. Even the worst serial killer in the nation's history is a real man, with problems and loved ones and feelings and so on. There are two sides to this – he is the same as us and we are the same as him. It is the latter that is the really difficult lesson to learn.

The whole Nedland's Monster sequence calls into question the existence of evil as an explanation for such actions. Quick's final attitude is that we are all the same, but some of us do what others only think of doing.

This attitude of tolerance is a characteristic of the novel. The novel doesn't pass judgement on any of the members of the Lamb and Pickles families.

THEMATIC CONCERNS

Life and Death

Human existence is presented as continuous, and as both physical and spiritual. Winton presents death very specifically, on two occasions, and in both cases the consciousness is uninterrupted by death. Fish still exists, after death, to put it that way. Existence operates concurrently on physical and spiritual levels. This is the central theme of the novel.

This view of existence is demonstrated through the story of Fish Lamb, who 'dies', then is brought back into the physical world. Though, as his brother Quick recognises, 'not all of Fish Lamb had come back.'(p 32) So, for the bulk of the novel, Fish Lamb is in a sense 'separated from himself.' His is a quest for wholeness – to return to the water and be complete. It appears that he is not free to do this until certain aspects of the life of his family have been put in order – until they are ready to let him go, if you like.

At the end of the novel, major signs of this 'readiness' are Quick and Rose uniting the Lambs and Pickles in marriage and through the birth of Wax Harry, and Oriel's gradual return to the family, symbolised in the end by the folding of her tent. So, when Fish returns to the water, this time no one pulls him back.

The Family

Winton upholds the family as the source of love on earth and as a refuge from the difficulties of life.

He deals with this theme through the juxtaposition of the Lambs and the Pickles, and through their ultimate unity in Rose, Quick and Wax Harry.

The Lambs

- An identity as well as a name
- A team, with Oriel as leader
- Lester as the heart of the family. He sees himself in terms of being a father.
- Lost faith which must be overcome in acceptance
- Oriel's move back into the house represents a return to the family and an acceptance of things as they are

The Pickles

- Five individuals with the same name, little sense of family
- Neither Sam nor Dolly perform the roles in the family traditionally expected of parents
- Animosity between Rose and Dolly which is resolved when Dolly tells Rose the truth
- Belief in luck, which is pagan
- Really only become a family when they are joined with the Lambs

In the end these two contrasting and disparate groups unite under the power of the house and the birth of Wax Harry to become the 'Cloudstreet' family.

On page 303, Quick asks Lester 'So what...what d'you live for?' and Lester laughs and replies, simply 'The family, Quick.' In *Cloudstreet*, the family is the final refuge from the sometime miseries and confusions of life.

Faith and Acceptance

The Lambs lose their faith in the Christian God when Fish drowns and returns incomplete. Oriel becomes alienated from Fish and from the family in her anger at God. It is her interference with the will of God that causes Fish's 'separation' in the first place and causes him to be unable to recognise her. Quick's disappearance is another blow to her. This alienation is represented physically by her moving out into the tent

Lester's belief in the knife (the knife never lies) and his bouts of gambling and infidelity can all be seen as stemming from the family's loss of faith. The belief in luck is a pagan belief. They become people adrift in life, and none of them can pray. Lester, though, always holds to the belief in the family.

Oriel's prawning trip with Quick and her dancing with Dolly at the wedding indicate a shift towards acceptance, which, along with the birth of Wax Harry, allows Fish the freedom to leave and be reunited with his other self. The fact that Quick lets him go and no one else tries to intervene is an indication of acceptance.

The novel suggests that life goes on and that we must accept things as they are. This theme focuses on Oriel as she wants to believe that she can control things.

Place

A sense of place, being where you belong, is important in all of Winton's novels. In *Cloudstreet*, Fish belongs in the water and once he is separated from his spiritual self in the prawning accident he craves to return to the water and be reunited with his other self.

For the other characters, the house at No 1 Cloud Street, known in the district as the one word entity Cloudstreet, is their place. The house is an organism with a life and a history of its own. While Fish is the most attuned to this, Lester, Sam, Quick, Oriel and Rose all on occasions say things that indicate their awareness of the life of the house.

Both Quick and Rose try to leave Cloudstreet and are forced back. When they have the opportunity to finally leave (the new house in the suburbs) they decide not to, accepting that they and Harry belong at Cloudstreet.

Sam decides not to sell the place to developers and so the house facilitates the unity of the Pickles and Lambs into the 'Cloudstreets', if you like. The house's demons from the past are exorcised by the birth of Wax Harry, who embodies the unity.

The various appearances of the black man help encourage the characters to return to the place of Cloudstreet. The black man's appearances also introduce Aboriginal culture into the novel. Place is an important aspect of Aboriginal culture, and the novel puts an equal amount of significance on it as does Aboriginal culture. No one in the novel can be content if they are not in the right physical environment – in the right place.

Luck

Sam Pickles believes that luck is a determining force operating in life. He refers to the 'shifty shadow of God' to describe the feeling that he gets sometimes that something is going to happen. He gets this feeling on the morning of the day that he loses his fingers. But Sam's belief systems having nothing to do with God – 'luck' is a pagan value.

Sam's life is mostly a testament to the power of bad luck, especially in terms of gambling. In this way, Sam is juxtaposed to Oriel, who believes that nothing in life should be left up to luck and that everything can be controlled. By the end of the novel, life has taught her otherwise.

Sam's one great piece of good luck, as it turns out, comes from bad luck to his cousin 'lucky' Joel who has a heart attack and dies, leaving his old city dwelling at No 1 Cloud Street to his Sam. This, and Sam's inability to provide for his family in any other way, leads the Pickles to the city and Cloudstreet, and to having the Lambs as tenants.

Winton judges Sam to the extent that he implies that life shouldn't just be left to luck and that the existence of luck isn't an excuse for weakness and laziness. But Winton also tells us that Oriel needs to understand that she isn't in control of all things.

The novel demonstrates the existence of luck, but not that life is random. Life has its ups and downs in *Cloudstreet*, but in the end the novel upholds a belief in destiny. Things happen because they are meant to. People end up where they are meant to be.

Identity

Large sections of the narrative of *Cloudstreet* are devoted to Quick's and Rose's quests for identity. They both seek identity outside of the family and away from the 'place' Cloudstreet. They are both running away from an image of themselves that they want to deny.

Quick seems comfortable in the rural setting and achieves an adult status for himself, as well as experiencing his first love affair. At first he resists the black man's attempt to encourage him to go back to Cloudstreet, but eventually he has no choice as Earl and May drive him home when he starts to glow.

Rose grows as a person, in self-esteem and confidence through her venture into the city and her relationship with Toby Raven. At the literary soiree, she could have gone along with Toby in the mocking of her family and the living circumstances of Cloudstreet, but she has the sense of herself by then to stand up for them by leaving.

In the end, Quick and Rose find their sense of themselves through their relationships with each other and with the family(s). And they can only be themselves in the right place – Cloudstreet itself is their home, their destiny and their place.

Guilt

The theme of guilt is examined through Quick's and Lester's sense of guilt for what has happened to Fish. This is especially poignant with regard to Quick, as he was only eleven years old at the time and in the presence of his father who naturally would accept the responsibility for his sons' safety.

Quick's guilt causes him to fix his mind on human suffering and evil in the pictures and clippings that he has on the wall of his room at Cloudstreet. The death of Wogga McBride adds to his sense of, as Oriel puts it, being 'a survivor' and the guilt associated with that. Is it more difficult to be the one who survives? It is this guilt which causes Quick to run away.

Once he has returned, Quick is, I think by anyone's standards, a very good brother indeed. Quick's guilt over Fish is resolved, ironically, by not preventing him from going to the water and drowning at the end of the novel. It is an act of love, to allow Fish to go to where he needs to be.

Lester carries the burden of adult responsibility for Fish's accident. He also assumes that he must be responsible for Quick leaving home. He battles on, holding the family together as best he can, and trying to keep everyone smiling (and singing and dancing and spinning knives and telling jokes).

The occasion when Rose interrupts Sam when he is contemplating suicide suggests that after all there might be some sense of responsibility in him for the state of things in his family.

The novel sees things as just happening and doesn't ascribe guilt for what happens in life. Individual humans feel guilt as a result of their wish that things might not be as they are. Acceptance is really the remedy for guilt.

LANGUAGE ANALYSIS

Technique of Narration

Winton's choice of technique of narration is the most significant device that he uses in the novel. It is best to read the novel as narrated by the spiritual Fish, the part of Fish Lamb that did not come back.

The story is told in the moment of drowning: 'having known the story for just a moment'. (p 2) and 'as long as it took to tell you all this' (p 424). This device picks up on the commonplace notion of one's life passing before one's eyes in the moment of death. In this case, Fish's life and the life of the Pickles as well are included. If human life is a quest for understanding, then Winton tells us that the understanding will come at the end.

You can look at it as the spiritual ('dead') Fish addressing the physical ('alive') Fish. That it is Fish addressing us is most explicit in sections such as 'Burning the Man', 'Down into the Light Samson Lamb', 'Heat of the Night', 'Soon' and 'The Moon, Sun, Stars'. In these sections we also see Fish's separation into the spiritual and the physical beings most clearly.

For example, in 'Soon' (p 420) the spiritual narrator Fish addresses the physical Fish 'Can you see me, Fish...? Then: 'The earth slips away, Fish, and soon, soon you'll be yourself, and we'll be us; you and me. Soon!' The spiritual Fish reassures the physical Fish that his agony of displacement is nearly over and soon the two will become one.

For the bulk of the narrative, the physical Fish is 'you' or addressed as 'Fish' or 'Samson Lamb' but in the final moment it is 'Me' (p 424) indicating that the two have reunited.

Few readers will have a full understanding of this technique of narration on first reading, but once you understand, it makes sense.

Style

The novel utilises the conventions of oral storytelling. It is a yarn, told by Fish. So, it is rambling and loose in structure. Sometimes it heads down diversions from the main story just for the hell of it or because they are amusing. Characteristically of yarns, it is the reader's job to differentiate the more important from the less important.

For all the potential solemnity of its themes, the novel is very funny. Winton uses humour to present humans as being lovable in spite of their faults. The novel gets its warmth from its sense of humour. An example of humour is the section 'Put Yer Dukes Up, Woman!' (p 399–401) where Oriel interrupts Lon and Pansy making love in order to get him to load the truck. When she isn't satisfied with the job, she spanks him with a fence paling and when he challenges her to fight, she knocks him down with one punch. The section is very funny and it does tell us some things about Oriel. (She can fight!)

The novel is full of Christian imagery and references.

The figure of the black man as an angel reconciles Christianity with Aboriginal culture, especially its sense of place.

The fish is the ancient and recent contemporary symbol of Christianity.

Quick goes away and comes back, as The Prodigal Son in the Bible. Both Rose and Oriel also try to leave the family and are 'prodigal' for a time.

The pig speaking is said by Lester to be 'Pentecostal', referring to speaking in tongues or claiming to be making direct contact with God.

Fish is Christ-like in his effect on others – especially that his death opens the way for Oriel to return to the family and the place where she belongs.

The two occurrences of 'miracle' fishing, Quick catching fish in Earl's boat and Oriel and Quick catching masses of prawns out of season are Biblical references to the disciples being fishermen and the sense of plenitude in the world.

The final scene where Dolly and Oriel fold away the tent and re-enter the house is compared to Matthew 27:51 where Christ's death causes a rent in the curtain of the temple so that all could enter.

Further Biblical References are listed and discussed are discussed in detail in the section below 'Christianity in *Cloudstreet*.'

Australian Style

The novel's 'Australianness' is often commented on. So often, in fact, that it is difficult to deny that it strikes readers as Australian. What does this mean?

It is written in Australian idiom, using many unique Australian expressions and colloquialisms.

- The second sentence of the novel contains the words 'skylarking and chiaking', meaning 'mucking about'. These are Australian slang words of the 1940s.
- On page 7: 'Rose...watched her brothers and a whole mob of other kids chucking bombies off the end of the jetty' and 'Ted! Chub! Carn, it's late.'
- Page 31: '...the most awful sickfeeling is in him like his flesh is turned to pus and his heart to shit.'
- Through to page 422: '...watch Lester dance his silly longlegged jig while half choking on his roast chook... and even Chubb is up off his arse and dancing.'

Only an Australian could have written these lines.

Winton's use of the Australian vernacular is authentic but it is also part of the novel's nostalgia for the 1940s and 1950s. This language is what gives the novel its warmth and it contributes greatly to our affection for the characters. A lot of the humour in the novel derives from the language.

Characters

The characters are very Australian.

Lester is an Australian stereotype – the Dad who is the biggest kid in the family. Good hearted, but a bit of a duffer who tends to create problems in an attempt to solve them. He is similar to a stereotypical father, seen in a lot of advertising.

Sam is another stereotype – the seemingly hopeless gambler and the man who is scared of his wife.

Quick is associated with a lot of so-called Australian characteristics – self-reliant, down to earth, man of few words, unpretentious, loves simple pleasures and natural surroundings.

Chub, Fish and Quick have very Australian nick-names. ('Quick' because he's slow.)

The *themes* of the novel are universal, but the *style* of it is Australian.

STRUCTURE

The novel is a saga. It follows the story of a family (in this case two families that become one) over some twenty years. Within this there is a long series of episodes that might focus on one character or another. So the novel shows the progress of the individuals within the family as well as the family as a unit.

The opening and closing sections are untitled and constitute a kind of parenthesis around the novel. The opening (or prologue) is in fact the ending - 'Moon, Sun, Stars' (pp 422–424). A figure, whom we later understand to be Fish, returns to the water to find wholeness. The shift from third to second person in the final lines of the prologue seems to broaden Fish's experience to make it that of all humanity. It is also the spiritual Fish addressing the physical Fish. The final word of 'Moon, Sun, Stars' is 'Me' indicating the reunification of the two Fish's.

The body of the novel is divided into ten numbered 'chapters' and each chapter is divided into many sections with names. These sections vary a great deal in length. This structure enables Winton to juggle a large number of narrative strands at the same time. He is able to move between the 'stories' of Quick, Rose, Lester, Sam, the house, Fish's internal monologues or conversations with himself, the black man and so on. This is one of the things that makes *Cloudstreet* a 'big' novel following many strands of stories over a period of over twenty years. The reader has the sense of encountering life in all its glory and grime.

The ending, or epilogue, is a kind of new beginning made mostly out of acceptance, as two women, clearly Oriel and Dolly, fold the tent and end Oriel's separation from the house and the family.

Significantly, no names are stated, as these could be any people anywhere – these actions are to be played out over and over. There are many points being made: death is not an ending, existence is continuous, acceptance is our only option, the family our refuge.

CHRISTIANITY IN *CLOUDSTREET*

Readers who are familiar with Christianity and the Christian Bible will have noticed a range of Biblical references in *Cloudstreet*. These have led some readers to want to develop a 'Christian reading' of the novel. This is to see the novel as deliberately interweaving these Biblical references in order to uphold Christian beliefs through the novel.

Following is a list of some documented Biblical references in the novel:

- At the very end of the novel, Oriel and Dolly fold Oriel's tent and she returns to the house – 'then they went inside the big old house whose door stood open.' (p426) Through Fish dying, the door has been opened for Oriel to return to the house and family. In the Bible, Matthew 27:45, Mark 15:38 and Luke 23:45, upon Jesus' death the curtain of the temple was torn in two, opening up the way for all people to enter. Thus giving all people access to God and the church.

- 'they leapt into the boat of their own accord' (p 216) At this point Quick is fishing whilst on a break from working with his uncle. In the Bible, Jesus performs the miracle of the fish catch at Luke 5: 4-11. The disciples have been fishing and have caught nothing until Jesus tells them to lay their nets down again and they are filled to overflowing. This is an image of plenitude, the generosity of God's grace. Another image of this occurs when Quick goes prawning with Oriel and they catch an impossible number of prawns out of season.

- 'They drink and eat…the wine and bread seem inexhaustible' (p 209) Here the Black Man provides food and drink for himself and Quick. In the Bible Jesus fed a crowd of five thousand with five loaves and two fish, and there were twelve full baskets left over – Matthew 14: 13-21. Lyn McCredden, in an essay on Winton's novel wrote, "Some critics do not like Winton's sacred, seeing it as too narrowly Christian. However, conversely, it might be argued by readers that sacredness in Winton is given a particularly earthy (or perhaps sea-washed) breadth; and that the sacred in Cloudstreet is working – poetically, humorously, and in the curve of the narrative – towards new possibilities, new ways of imagining how to belong and to make meaning in contemporary Australia."(Dreams of Belonging: Tim Winton's Cloudstreet Teacher Resource http://readingaustralia.com.au/Secondary/Cloudstreet/Essay.aspx)
- 'He saw the figure of a man walking upon the water' (p 216) The Black Man is the person walking on the water. Jesus walked on water, Matthew 14: 22-33.

- Quick, as in the parable of the prodigal son, leaves the family and eventually returns. Lester comments 'Hardly a fatted calf is it?' when Quick gets burnt eggs for breakfast the next morning. In the Bible, the father holds a big feast, killing the fatted calf, when the son returns. (Luke 15: 11-32).

- Rose, is in a sense 'the prodigal daughter' in that she deserts her origins and social class in going with Toby Raven, an educated writer. She then develops the dream of having a new house of their own. Eventually, like the Bible's prodigal son, she returns to Cloudstreet.

Oriel is also a kind of prodigal, in that she moves out of the house proper into a tent in the backyard. Her move back in at the very end of the novel is the final image of peace and reconciliation.

- The pig's speech is 'Pentecostal' – the pig is 'talking in tongues'. Lester and Quick both accept that the pig speaks, but only Fish can converse with it. At Harry's birth, the pig is 'like the voice of God Himself'. (p 385) It cries out in celebration at the end to the suffering of the past of the house. Thus, Harry's birth unites the Pickles and the Lambs in another sense beyond Rose and Quick's marriage. Harry is the embodiment of the unity of Cloudstreet and he purges the ghosts of the history of the house.

All of these references enhance the sense of the connection between the Bible and *Cloudstreet*.

There emerges a strong suggestion that Fish is like Christ, he dies so that others can be saved, especially Quick and Oriel. There are Christ-links to the Black Man as well, though it is more often argued that he is an angel – perhaps an agent of Fish/Christ. His role is to make sure that Quick does return to the Lambs and that all proceeds as it should and that Fish can return to the water and his self.

The novel also upholds the Protestant work ethic where better things come to those who work for them. The value of truth, of not 'bearing false witness' is also upheld. Within both families, wounds are healed and acceptance grows through the truth being revealed.

Overall, Winton depicts a world where God will provide. Both the Pickles and especially the Lambs are at times down and vulnerable, but God always provides in some way. Even Sam is let off the hook when he wins enough at two-up to pay his gambling debts.

Whether you see the novel as a 'Christian' novel is up to you.

Winton can be seen as presenting a version of heaven at the end of the novel. Fish has arrived at the place and time where he belongs and he can go to be reunited with his other self and with God.

OTHER BELIEF SYSTEMS IN *CLOUDSTREET*

It is certainly possible to develop a Christian reading of *Cloudstreet,* but there is evidence of alternative belief systems in the novel as well. I will begin by discussing some aspects of the novel that don't sit so well with the Christian reading.

1. The Ghosts

The house Cloudstreet is populated by the ghosts of the young Aboriginal women who had lived there (in virtual captivity) earlier in the century. Fish is aware of their existence all the time and other characters occasionally. Christianity holds the view that upon death the soul flies from this world. The Christian belief system does not allow for the existence of ghosts in the house.

2. Cloudstreet as being alive

The house itself is a living, breathing organism. Christianity does not encompass the idea of what we call inanimate objects having a life or a soul. Cloudstreet the house is like a character in the novel. Its restlessness and unsettled nature is purged with the birth of Wax Harry.

3. The Nedlands Monster

Quick's initial view of the Nedlands Monster as the embodiment of evil is consistent with Christianity in that Christianity is a belief system that supports the idea of the existence of evil. Quick, though, gradually comes to understand that the Monster is really just a man, that men like him are merely doing what others think about but don't do. Quick, in the end, feels sorry for him.

The novel itself, upholds this latter view and offers a view of criminality based on psychological motives. The Monster isn't evil, he's pathetic and sick. The novel's view is Christian in the sense that it is forgiving, but non-Christian in the sense that it challenges the very notion of the existence of evil.

4. The Description of Fish's Death

There is very much the sense at the end that Fish, as well as being reunited with himself, is being spread out into the whole universe. Also, it is based on the uniting of the body Fish with the spiritual Fish. The Christian notion of death is the opposite of this. The soul separates from the body and goes to God. At the end of the novel, Fish becomes himself and everything. 'Being Fish Lamb. Perfectly. Always. Everyplace. Me.' (p 424) It is a consummation of individuality and boundlessness. It is a paradox to suggest that Fish becomes both himself and everything at once. The Christian view of death is simpler and not based on this paradox.

Other Belief Systems Evident in *Cloudstreet*

Paganism

Sam's belief in 'the shifty shadow' and 'Lady Luck' are pagan beliefs, deriving from value systems outside of Christianity. Dolly, Rose, Quick and Lester (with the spinning knife) also express a belief in the power of sheer luck. If you think, as I do, that the novel itself holds up the idea of luck, then this weakens the argument that the novel is entirely Christian, as luck is a pagan notion not based on the existence of God. Astrology may also seen to be referenced in the symbol of Pisces, the two way fish.

Some of the ideas in this following section are drawn from an article by Watt, G. (2005). "Shadows without light: zen and blackfellas in Cloudstreet." NUCB Journal of Language, Culture and Communication, 6(1), 59-70.

Zen Buddhism

According to Zen Buddhism, the individual is the whole universe and the universe is a representation of the individual. It is like a microcosm/macrocosm paradigm. This idea is consistent with the way Winton describes Fish's death on page 424. Fish rejoins himself and at once, becomes a part of everything. He is himself and the universe at once.

The notion of Nirvana is one that incorporates the self into the universe. Nirvana relies on the interconnectedness of things. This idea is also consistent with Winton's writing about Fish's death on page 424.

The first of the Buddha's 'noble truths' is that life is suffering. The novel *Cloudstreet* bears this out well.

Sam suffers the loss of his fingers and lives a life based on the belief that luck is everything and that his own will always be bad.

Dolly's early life is dominated by incest, leading her to seek affection through promiscuous sex. Her relationships are abusive and dysfunctional. She hates herself and the family around her.

Oriel grew up supporting her father after the death of the rest of her family. Her favourite son was intellectually impaired when he nearly drowned. The fact that she 'saved' him on the beach and thought she had been blessed with a miracle makes the suffering greater. She feels betrayed by God. To Oriel, life is a battle.

Lester suffers the same loss of faith after Fish's accident. He regards himself as untrustworthy and responsible for what happened to Fish. His wife moves out of the house and lives in a tent.

Quick blames himself for what happened to Fish. He sees misery and suffering in life wherever he looks. He seeks redemption by running away. He believes in evil.

Rose's central suffering comes back to her day of trauma. This is the day when her father lost his fingers and she was sent to fetch her mother. She arrives at the pub to find Dolly in bed with a stranger. She gets no love from her mother.

Zen thought begins with place. The idea of place is central to *Cloudstreet*. All the characters are searching for the right place to be. Quick and Rose both go on pilgrimages to find the place where they belong (separately and together) and they finally end up back in Cloudstreet as their place. The older generation decide to stay in Cloudstreet on the night of the dinner before Rose and Quick go away. Fish is searching for the water – his place.

Aboriginal Culture

The notion of place is equally important in Aboriginal culture. The Aboriginals believe that they belong to their place, to the land.

Also, the idea of the life in inanimate objects is central to them. This is called 'animism', the idea that a house could have a spirit.

Remember that the black man appears to Sam and tells him that it would be a terrible thing to sell Cloudstreet to developers who would tear the house down.

Aboriginal culture also contains the idea of humans having animal totems. The black man becomes a bird at the end when he is leaving as he can see that things are now as they should be. Samson Lamb becomes Fish, his natural environment is the water. It is his home.

Aboriginal culture is based on the interconnectedness of things, as is the novel. In the novel, nothing happens in isolation, everything is part of a process to bring everyone together so that Fish can return to himself through the water.

We do not know whether Tim Winton has deliberately used these references to Zen and to Aboriginal culture in the novel. The main thing that I would put to you is that these features weaken the argument that *Cloudstreet* is merely a Christian treatise on life.

The novel clearly contains references to the Bible and much of what happens is consistent with Christian beliefs. But there are aspects that are more consistent with other alternative belief systems, such as Zen Buddhism and Aboriginal culture.

It seems to me that Winton has not based his novel on one particular philosophy or set of beliefs. He is interested in the powerful notion of the Christian God and the consistency of that with some of the features of human life. Life is controlled by forces that are bigger than the individuals who are caught up in them. But in the end he tells his story as he sees it as happening. It is not based on any particular pre-arranged set of beliefs.

VARIED READINGS

If you are studying *Cloudstreet* in Module B of the NSW Advanced English course, you must read and respond to your text. You must also demonstrate your understanding of the fact that the text can be read in a number of different ways. Three readings is a good number for your purposes. There are two basic sources of 'readings':

- Critical articles about *Cloudstreet*
- Readings of *Cloudstreet*, from a particular context, for example a feminist or psychoanalytical reading

Always remember that the most important reading is your own. What you should do is use these other readings as approaches that help in the development of your own reading.

I will summarise some readings of *Cloudstreet* here for you. If they sound interesting to you, you can look them up for yourself.

"Go Home said the Fish" A study of Tim Winton's *Cloudstreet*, by Michael McGirr

Reference: *Meanjin* Vol 56 No 1 1997 (pp56-66)

Meanjin is an Australian literary journal.

- McGirr begins by pointing out that Winton wrote most of *Cloudstreet* while on an Australia Council funded stay in Paris. Other parts were written in Greece and in Ireland.
- He argues that *Cloudstreet*, partly because of this, is a

nostalgic book. But its nostalgia is not so much for a place (Australia) but for a time - the 1940s and 50s – the era immediately before Winton's own birth. He notes all the references in the novel to commercial products (velvet soap, fridgidaire, Porphyry Pearl), places and expressions (zacs, deaners and drongo). McGirr claims that it is a nostalgia for a time of greater moral security (the difference between right and wrong was more clearly defined).

- He notes that the characters in the novel are based on Winton's own family – his grandmother did live in a tent, his grandfather was an entertainer and his father was a policeman. So the era he is harkening after is the one of his grandparents and parents, the one that he has heard about in family legend.
- McGirr sees the novel in terms of nostalgia, a longing for home. Home can take a number of forms.
- For Fish, home is the water, the place where his 'other' self is – the self that he was separated from at the time of the near drowning (pp 29–32). For Lester it is the memory of being carried to safety by his own father during a storm. For Oriel it is, according to McGirr, the longing 'for all the broken pieces of her life to flow back together' – the death of her mother that turned her into a 'leftover' in her father's new family. For Quick it is Cloudstreet, a return guided by the black man. For Rose it is Cloudstreet too, after the failure of her relationship with Toby. For Dolly, it is reconciliation with her daughter Rose.
- McGirr says: 'In every case, the call home is a call to completion.'
- McGirr's view on the technique of narration is that Fish is

separated into two at the moment of the near drowning and that the narrator is one Fish speaking to the other Fish. The book is in fact one moment, the moment of Fish's return to the other part of himself – 'as long as it took to tell you all this'. (p 424)

- He also sees landscape, architecture and people as being all tied together in the book. Number 1 Cloudstreet stands for Australia and it is a living, breathing being.

McGirr's view of the novel is that it is principally about going 'home' and the desire for 'completion'. Fish is split into two, so for him completion is rejoining his two selves. For all the characters, completion is being what and where they belong.

You should apply the ideas in this summary to your own thoughts about *Cloudstreet*. Answer these questions for yourself:

1. What aspects of McGirr's argument seem to be valid?

2. Are there any aspects which conflict with my own view?

3. Does his argument throw any new light on the novel for me?

When you write about *Cloudstreet*, give McGirr credit for his ideas and work them into your overall view of the novel.

"Tim Winton Writing the Feminine" by Elizabeth Guy
Reference: *Women-Church* 19, Spring 1996 (pp 31–37)

Women-Church is a feminist theology journal.

- Winton's novels are dominated by male quests and male narrators.
- Yet women are absolutely central to his books.
- Women are the 'other', the feminine is erotic, desired and feared.
- Woman is both 'whore' and 'madonna'. This means that women are seen, at once, as sexual beings and images of purity, placed on a pedestal.
- The longing for the sea and the longing for place are both manifestations of the desire for the feminine.
- At first, the women in *Cloudstreet* seem like stereotypes – Dolly is the promiscuous alcoholic, Rose the inhibited anorexic and Oriel the domineering sexless matron. But the women are gradually seen as strong compared to the weak and inert men.
- Guy calls this: 'the rupturing of the patriarchal structures'. She is referring to traditional family structure where the male is the boss and principal breadwinner. Both Sam and Lester are weak in their own ways, and neither is a successful breadwinner.
- Winton ruptures the stereotype of women being the passive recipients of sex. Dolly uses sex as her currency (she gets what she wants through sex), Rose pursues Quick and Oriel wields power by removing herself from the marital bed and moving to the tent.
- Dolly and Oriel are the pivotal points of their two families. They break convention when they dance together at Rose and Quick's wedding (and they

symbolise the union of the two families.) They break conventions about women and they also challenge the power of the father.

- Rose becomes both communion and country for Quick (p 314).
- Oriel is the barrier to Fish returning to the water and becoming fully man.
- The traditional vulnerability of the female has been transferred to the male.

Guy writes from a feminist context. She sees the novel in terms of power structures and recognises that there is a transfer of power from the male to the female. Guy's terminology gives you a way of discussing this issue from a feminist viewpoint. Briefly, her claim is that although at first glance the novel seems to be more about males, the feminine is at least as important and the novel in fact challenges gender orthodoxies.

You should apply the ideas in this summary to your own thoughts about *Cloudstreet*. Answer these questions for yourself:

1. What aspects of Guy's argument seem to be valid?

2. Are there any aspects which conflict with my own view?

3. Does her argument throw any new light on the novel for me?

"What Can Be Read, and What Can Only Be Seen in Tim Winton's Fiction"
by Andrew Taylor

Reference: Australian Literary Studies Vol 7 No 4 1996

- The sea figures prominently in all of Winton's fiction. In *Cloudstreet*, he utilises the fact that Perth is built on an estuary, so that 'the water (is) almost entirely held in the city's embrace.' Almost, except for the fact that the estuary is part of the Swan River and therefore subject to its currents. The idea is that the city tries to hold the river but it can't. The city represents civilisation, the river is a force that cannot be civilised.
- The water exercises a (literally) fatal attraction for Fish Lamb.
- One cannot ignore the significance of his name. Both the fish and the lamb conventionally signify Christ.
- Death and the river/sea 'are inextricably intertwined' in *Cloudstreet*.
- On the occasion when Quick and Fish row the boat that Lester has bought back to Nedlands, Quick has an experience where they seem to be floating in the sky – 'There's only sky out there, above and below, everywhere to be seen.' (p114). This is reminiscent of the passage in the Bible where God divides the firmament (Genesis 1.2). It is as though they have sailed back to a state before time, in a state where heaven is not divided from earth.
- Likewise, when Fish drowns the second time, he leaves the linear movement of time and arrives at a transcendent timelessness and placelessness in which the self and the universe are one: 'Perfectly. Always. Everyplace. Me.' (p424).

- It is a mode of knowing, beyond language. It is vision. Winton pushes his words to express something beyond words.
- The women in the novel are practical and tend to be the ones who keep things going, while the men are the ones 'looking beyond the horizon' to the imaginary.

You should apply the ideas in this summary to your own thoughts about *Cloudstreet*. Answer these questions for yourself:

1. What aspects of Taylor's argument seem to me to be valid?

2. Are there any aspects which conflict with my own view?

3. Does his argument throw any new light on the novel for me?

Gender

You could also develop an argument based on the difference between what Taylor says about gender and what Guy says. Guy says the women are stronger than the men, that there is a transfer of power in the novel from the traditional position of the men, to the women. Sam loses it when he loses his 'working hand' fingers, and Lester loses it when Oriel 'saves' Fish when Lester couldn't and this is exacerbated when Oriel runs the shop and moves into the tent. She also claims that Rose takes the upper hand in the relationship with Quick.

Taylor sees this phenomenon in a different light. He sees the women as more down-to-earth and practical, and the men as dreamers, visionaries, 'looking beyond the horizon'. He doesn't see it in terms of power. You need both kinds of people to function, so they complement each other. It would be fair to say, though, that Taylor's view gives the status to men, whereas Guy's gives it to women.

Adaptations for Stage and TV (Mini-Series)

The late Nick Enright and Justin Monjo adapted this novel for the stage. The play of *Cloudstreet* opened in 1998 in Sydney under the direction of Neil Armfield. The play was then taken to Perth, Melbourne, London, Dublin, New York and Washington DC. It is a lengthy adaptation at over five hours. The play attracted rave reviews around the world. The play is published by Currency Press.

'Nostalgia, Reconciliation or New National Myth?: The Adaptation of Cloudstreet to the Stage' is a commended 2006 academic article by Jack Teiwes, Australasian Drama Studies. If you have acccess to Questia you can access the whole article. Otherwise, read an extract. Teiwes acknowledges that the stage adaptation redefined *Cloudstreet* as a broad, contemporary address concerning the 'state of the nation' for Australia and an ideal for its future, including a politicised statement of Aboriginal Reconciliation. He saw the novel, however, as a family saga, defined by time and place and therefore, narrower and less symbolic in focus and meaning.

Also consider, *Cloudstreet* (2011 TV Mini-Series) Directed by Matthew Saville ... (6 episodes) It might be worth examining at least one episode closely and comparing it with the novel and one critical piece. Essie Davis plays Dolly Pickles, Stephen Curry plays Sam Pickles and Emma Booth plays their daughter Rose. Grass Roots' Geoff Morrell plays Lester Lamb, Kerry Fox is Oriel Lamb, Todd Lasance is Quick and Hugo Johnstone-Burt plays Fish. None of the original cast of the earlier stage adaptation by Nick Enright and Justin Monjo were cast. Winton himself and Ellen Fontana wrote the script for the TV mini-series.

http://www.middlemiss.org/matilda/2011/05/television-adaptaton-of-cloudstreet-by-tim-winton.html

The website above contains extracts from reviews of the Television mini-series, published in various newspapers.

By Perry Middlemiss on May 25, 2011

Reviews

Herald-Sun: "Cloudstreet is a big, risky move for Showcase. To ensure their survival, subscriber channels simply have to go the extra metre, producing original material good enough to belong on an even bigger screen and that's what Showcase has done. At the same time, it has taken on a novel so loved across a couple of generations of Australians that it potentially has set itself up for a fall. It won't happen this time, though."

The Australian: "The 1999 stage production brilliantly captured it in a very literal transformation. This miniseries does just as well not to be sucked into easy options -- cheesy nostalgia, overwrought visual effects or you-beaut Australiana -- that could have spoiled the visual rendering of a classic. Cloudstreet is fine, involving filmmaking that will meet impossible expectations, those of our own imaginations. The six hours begins grimly in the first two-hour episode, as it must, but soon opens into a delight that justice has been done to a grand novel."

http://content.foxtelmovies.com.au/cloudstreet/images/cloudstreet_makeup01.JPG

This website will provide you with many images on the making of the TV mini-series as well as notes on make-up, costume and set design. How faithfully do you think this visual form captures the plot, people and places of the original novel? Is the essence still present? What about the themes and main ideas, are they the same? Consider the golden cover of the Penguin, 2007 edition. Do you find it effective? Why or why not? How is lighting used in the mini-series? What does it convey?

The subtitle on the cover of the novel states, The Modern Australian Classic. Do you consider this to be the case? Justify your response. Might it also be said of the mini-series? Winton was partly responsible for writing the script for the mini-series. Is this significant? Why or why not? Does it make it a more authentic adaption?

DEVELOPING YOUR OWN READING OF *CLOUDSTREET*

Foundational to any critical study of the novel, are very close readings of the text. From such close reading, the opinions and interpretations of others can be evaluated. Here, a close study of 'prologue' (pp 1-3), 'Fish Lamb Comes Back' (pp 25–32) and 'Moon, Sun, Stars' (pp 422–424) is offered. Note that in each of these sections, Winton experiments with form, structure and / or person.

The Prologue (p 1-3)

The novel opens in second person: 'Will you look at us by the river!' Winton uses this technique to draw the reader into the novel. Here the use of second person reinforces the view that the novel is being narrated by one Fish to the other Fish. But no reader can really guess this at first reading. So, the other effect it has is to make the reader feel as though he/she is being addressed – it is us being invited to look at the family by the river. And, of course, this is true – the reader is being invited to read the story and learn about the people who are here at the river side.

The narration shifts into third person in the second paragraph and stays that way until the final paragraph of the Prologue. Fish becomes 'he' – 'He hears nothing but the water' (p 2). Life is depicted as a state of plenty. The relationship between the spirit world and the world of the living is established – 'look, even the missing are there, the gone and taken'. The use of third person narration can be read as indicating that in this section, the two fishes are already united and the 'he' in the passage is Fish's physical being, his body, if you like.

Winton uses a meaningful pun in 'Within a minute he'll have it, and it'll have him', a reference to death – it is what he wants and it will consume him. The 'flicker' and 'having known the story for just a moment' seem to be a reference to the commonplace notion of one's life passing before one's eyes at the moment of death – this is what Fish is about to experience (and what the reader is about to read.)

In the last paragraph Winton shifts back to second person, as though one Fish addresses the other. It also cleverly has the effect of positioning the reader as Fish. This is important because this is our destiny as humans, we will all experience this one day – that is one of the central messages of the novel. 'We' are Fish, the dying and the eternal, and we pity those who have to live on 'who go on down the close, foetid galleries of time and space without you.'

Fish Lamb Comes Back (pp 25–32)

'Lester and Oriel Lamb are Godfearing people' (p 26) but the events of the next few pages will shake their faith. Pages 29–32 describe the near (or partial) drowning of Fish under the Lamb's fishing nets. Reread them, and notice a few things.

It is Lester who inadvertently puts the light out, making the situation so much worse. He can't see where Fish is. On page 30, Winton shifts the narration suddenly from third person to first person, 'Oh, I remember', then back to third 'Fish feels death...' This can be read as one of the moments where Fish's narration becomes explicit. It is one Fish talking *to* the other, then talking *about* the other.

The lines 'and then he's away. / Away.', indicate the liberating and natural sensation of death.

Fish is free, but Oriel brings him back – 'he's slipping back and that gash in the grey recedes and darkness returns and pain'... and 'Fish begins to scream'. 'Never, never was there a sadder, more disappointed noise.' (p 31) This is why thereafter Fish refuses to recognise Oriel.

The Lambs drive to the church to celebrate, but Quick knows that 'not all of Fish Lamb had come back.'

Moon, Sun, Stars (p 424-424)

As McGirr (above) says, this passage describes the same event as the Prologue – Fish's return to the water, his death and his completion. The 400-odd pages in between have been the 'flicker', the life passing before the eyes at the moment of death. The black man knows that his job is done, so he leaves. This time Fish gets away, and Quick, who sees him, lets him go. 'Quick makes himself stop and already he's crying'.

As Fish rejoins his other self, the narration shifts back to first person: 'I'm Fish Lamb for those few seconds it takes to die'. Fish is integrated into the cosmos: 'Perfectly. Always. Everyplace. Me.' Winton uses single-word sentences so that each word, with its meaning, stands alone momentarily. It forces the reader to read slowly, taking each word separately. It drags the moment out so that the reader can savour and take it in.

The physical Fish's place is the water to which he must return, but the reintegrated Fish's place is 'Everyplace', the entire cosmos and beyond. The use of the word 'Me' at the end of 'Moon, Sun, Stars' is interesting because previously the narrator spiritual Fish had referred to the physical Fish as 'you', he even referred to 'us' (p 420) in 'Soon', indicating that there were two of them, separate.

Now in this moment of consummation, Fish is singular again, there is just one of him. So the narrator need only refer to 'Me' to include what had previously been 'us'.

In 'Dreams of Belonging: Tim Winton's Cloudstreet', Lyn McCredden writes, (http://readingaustralia.com.au/Secondary/Cloudstreet/Essay.aspx)

> *Some readers might want to emphasise only the (Christian? Marvelous? Sacred? Utopian?) hope of this novel, found in its narrative ending and its miraculous, comic and Romantic moments. They might want to dream, with the novel, of a place of belonging where there are 'No shadows, no ugliness, no hurtings, no falling down angry' (p. 530). But the novel draws us back, prompting us to acknowledge also the hauntings and the contradictions which bristle through Cloudstreet's marvelous, imagined world.*

Her words allude to the many and varied interpretations that have been offered by readers of this novel. Whether focussed on spirituality or magic realism; whether focussed on place (Australia) or a time (the era of the 1940s and 50s), whether viewed with a utopian or dystopian lens, what is important is that the novel represents life. What shines through, regardless of interpretation, is Hope. Winton has shown us the indomitable resilience of the human spirit. This is cause for celebration.

You are urged to find and read Lyn McCredden's 2013 essay for yourself.

One other text you may find helpful is Rossiter, R and Jacobs, L. (eds), *Reading Tim Winton*. Angus and Robertson, 1993.

THE ESSAY

The essay has been the subject of numerous texts and you should have the basic form well in hand. As teachers, the point we would emphasise would be to link the paragraphs both to each other and back to your argument (which should directly respond to the question). Of course ensure your argument is logical and sustained.

Make sure you use specific examples and that your quotes are accurate. To ensure that you respond to the question make sure you plan carefully and are sure what relevant point each paragraph is making. It is solid technique to actually 'tie up' each point by explicitly coming back to the question.

When composing an essay the basic conventions of the form are:

State your argument, outline the points to be addressed and perhaps have a brief definition.

↓

A solid structure for each paragraph is:

- Topic sentence *(the main idea and its link to the previous paragraph/argument)*
- Explanation / discussion of the point including links between texts if applicable.
- Detailed evidence *(Close textual reference- quotes, incidents and technique discussion.)*
- Tie up by restating the point's relevance to argument / question

↓

Summary of points
Final sentence that restates your argument

As well as this basic structure you will need to focus on:

Audience – for the essay the audience must be considered formal unless specifically stated otherwise. Therefore your language must reflect the audience. This gives you the opportunity to use the jargon and vocabulary that you have learnt in English. For the audience ensure your introduction is clear and has impact. Avoid slang or colloquial language including contractions (like doesn't, eg., etc.).

Purpose – the purpose of the essay is to answer the question given. The examiner evaluates how well you can make an argument and understand the module's issues and its text(s). An essay is solidly structured so its composer can analyse ideas. This is where you earn marks. It does not retell the story or state the obvious.

Communication – Take a few minutes to plan the essay. If you rush into your answer it is almost certain you will not make the most of the brief 40 minutes to show all you know about the question. More likely you will include irrelevant details that do not gain you marks but waste your precious time. Remember an essay is formal so **do not** do the following: story-tell, list and number points, misquote, use slang or colloquial language, be vague, use non sentences or fail to address the question.

MODEL ESSAY QUESTION AND PLAN

Question:

'No text can be responded to in the same way by all.'

Consider your prescribed text's ideas, language and form, and its reception in different contexts and forms.

In order to answer this question, you can draw on information in this book.

The text's ideas are found in the 'Thematic Concerns' section of the book.

Language and form are found in the 'Language' section and the part about the novel's 'Australianness.' The 'Structure' section deals with form.

The novel's reception in different contexts is seen in the 'Christianity and *Cloudstreet*' section and in the feminist reading by Guy.

The text has aspects of realism in place, time and family but there are other aspects which can be viewed as magic realism. The text, for some, may evoke a sense of nostalgia. Others may view the same aspects as social history. Some may see the novel as focussed on the human condition, others may see it contains a message of Hope, a celebration of resilience and tenacity.

Dealing with the question:

There is a quote before the actual question. The question does not instruct you to deal with the quote but you should at least refer to it as a 'theme' in your essay.

You need to refer to all the parts of the question, and there are four in all – ideas, language, form and reception in different contexts.

Your purpose is to determine whether there is enough that is 'universal' in *Cloudstreet* to see it being responded to in the same way in different contexts. Your discussion of the contexts could well find a lot of common ground, but you will probably be hard-pressed to argue that the novel will always be responded to in the same way in all contexts.

This module - Critical Study, often asks questions relating to the interpretations of others as well as your own response. The interpretations of others can be seen in adaptations and academic articles. Be sure to also formulate your own ideas, perhaps aligning your ideas with some readings and rejecting others.

Context is important to the way texts are received and responded to as context shapes our values and can affect meaning.

OTHER RESPONSES TO PRACTISE

1. 'The qualities of a text will determine its reception in different contexts.' Consider *Cloudstreet* in terms of ideas, language and form, and its reception in different contexts.

2. Consider how your text may be received in different ways in different contexts. What is your own critical response to it?

3. The ideas in a text are fluid and greatly affected by contexts. Do you agree with this statement in relation to *Cloudstreet*?

4. Contrast a reading of *Cloudstreet* which you find valid with one that you do not.

5. 'The context of the responder has more impact on the reading than the text itself.' Consider this claim with respect to *Cloudstreet*.

OTHER TYPES OF RESPONSES

It is crucial students realise that their responses in the examination, class and assessment tasks will NOT always be essays. This page is designed to give guidance with the different types of responses which are now required.

The response types covered in the exam may include some of the following:

- Writing in a role
- Journal/Diary Entry
- Brochure
- Point of view
- Radio interview
- Television interview
- Letter
- Feature article
- Speech
- Report
- Essay

Students should familiarise themselves with these types of responses and be able to write effectively in them. You should practice each one at some stage of your H.S.C. year.

For a comprehensive explanation of each of these writing forms with examples using the prescribed HSC texts see:

Pattinson, Bruce and Suzan, *Success in HSC Advanced English: A Practical Guide for Senior Students*